Fashionable Clothing

from the Sears Catalogs

Late 1960s

Desire Smith

Schiffer Publishing Ltd

4880 Lower Valley Road, Atglen, PA 19310 USA

Acknowledgments

Special thanks to Tammy Ward for all her hard work.

Copyright © 1998 by Desire Smith
Library of Congress Catalog Card Number: 98-85009

Designed by Blair Loughrey
Typeset in Normande BT/Futura BK BT

ISBN: 0-7643-0615-4
Printed in China
1 2 3 4

Published by Schiffer Publishing Ltd.
4880 Lower Valley Road
Atglen, PA 19310
Phone: (610) 593-1777; Fax: (610) 593-2002
E-mail: Info@schifferbooks.com
Please visit our web site catalog at
www.schifferbooks.com

This book may be purchased from the publisher.
Include $3.95 for shipping. Please try your bookstore first.
We are always looking for people to write books on new and related subjects. If you have an idea for a book please contact us at the above address.
You may write for a free catalog.

In Europe, Schiffer books are distributed by
Bushwood Books
6 Marksbury Avenue
Kew Gardens
Surrey TW9 4JF England
Phone: 44 (0) 20-8392-8585; Fax: 44 (0) 20-8392-9876
E-mail: info@bushwoodbooks.co.uk
Free postage in the UK. Europe: air mail at cost.

Contents

Introduction

The baby boomers had grown into rebellious teenagers, crushing the old values with their sheer numbers. Lacking the wisdom that often comes with age, the youth of the late 1960s approached the world with the simplistic notion that everything had to change. It was the best of times and it was the worst of times—politically, socially, and intellectually. Clothing styles reflect its intensity!

Two big fashion issues of the day were hair and skirt length. Many young men began wearing their hair long. Young women wore their hair in a myriad of hairstyles, some of which involved "add on" hair or "falls." False eyelashes and pale lipstick completed *the look*. Skirt lengths began to climb, and climb. The mini skirt was in fashion!

We can credit the 1960s with the demise of the hat. By the late 1960s the only hats offered by Sears were some wide ripple-brim sun hats, snap-brim straws, scarf-turbans, French berets, pillboxes, and "bubble" toques. We can also credit the late 1960s with the somewhat dubious emergence into fashion prominence of stretch pants. Stretch pants have metamorphosed into many forms since then, but we have never been without them! Styles such as the turtleneck tunic, the tank top, the long-tailed shirt, the pantskirt and pantjumper, the mini shirt (ties to show off the midriff), and flared-leg pants, all got their start in the late 1960s. The shift came into fashion, with all its variations, including the A-line shift and the pantshift. Let us not forget dome rings and chandelier earrings, knee-high boots and dropped waistlines, and the belted and shimmery acetate satin swimwear.

It was the age of double-knit polyester, late day stockings in the *point d'esprit* pattern, short gloves, polka-dots, windowpane plaids and ginghams, skimmer dresses, tent dresses, and vests of all descriptions. And everything, but everything, came in a kaleidoscope of color—hot orange, violet, pink, ginger, neon stripes, paisleys, and bold floral prints and plaids. It was the beginning of "flower power."

Vintage clothing from the late 1960s is popular today with collectors who enjoy wearing the styles, and with fashion designers who use the styles for inspiration. *Fashionable Clothing from the Sears Catalogs, Late 1960s,* focuses on wearable, collectible vintage clothing and accessories. The Sears catalogs provide the basis for a comprehensive study of the fashions of this period. There is no guessing as to the dates of the clothing. We know the exact dates. The descriptions in the catalogs are unsurpassed in terms of detail and accuracy. Not only do the descriptions help collectors to understand the styles of the period, they also give a complete analysis of the textiles used.

It is difficult for us to imagine the extreme attention to detail that was necessary to produce the Sears catalogs. Without the aid of computers, with word processing programs and "spell checks," rows of copy editors sat working quietly on the descriptions for the catalogs, descriptions designed to describe and sell the clothing. Colloquialisms of the late 1960s, such as "real cool," "jazzy," "swinging," "groovy," and "psychedelic" are used to enhance descriptions. Although Sears shows apparel for every market, from glamorous to practical, *Fashionable Clothing from the Sears Catalogs, Late 1960s* showcases the most collectible, trendy garments and accessories from the period. The apparel we find in the late 1960s Sears catalogs is not high fashion, but the Sears' buyers had an incredible "eye" for fashion. During the late 1960s Sears catalogs began to look more like fashion magazines, showing fewer images on a page, and accessories to enhance the garments modeled.

This book emphasizes fashions for women, but also includes examples of collectible fashions for men and children. Author's comments, designed to clarify and enhance, are interspersed with descriptive captions throughout the book, and a current value guide is placed next to the original Sears' prices. Late 1960s fashions are perhaps the most colorful and diverse in fashion history. Fortunately for the many avid collectors, these garments are still relatively easy to find.

Chapter One

Gowns, Dresses, Shifts, Suits, Skirts, and Shirts

Dressy clutch in faille or vinyl. Rayon-lined. $4 [$18-20] **Cage dress** of Rayon chiffon over luxurious crepe sheath of acetate and rayon; lined. Back has bowed, V-collar; zipper. $20 [$55-60] **Peek-a-boo swing along** shift with open, lacy-effect cotton knit over crepe of acetate and rayon. $16 [$45-50] **Bowed-band** of acetate and rayon crepe dress. Acetate taffeta lining. $13 [$45-50] **Side buttons** trim crinkle crepe of polyester and rayon. Front yoke, zips in back. $15 [$40-45]

Note: Shorter lengths tend to be more desirable than the long-length late 1960s gowns.

Whirl-about dress in a subtly-ribbed fabric of rayon and acetate. Bodice iced with overlay of white cotton lace. Long length: $23 [$40-45] Street length: $23 [$50-55] **Dreamy drifts** of white lace in acetate and nylon, acetate satin ribbon and bow. Long length: $22 [45-50] Street length: $20 [$50-55]

Top row: Skimmer. White dots printed on black crepe of acetate and rayon bonded to acetate tricot. Cotton lace trim; back zipper. $12 [$18-20] **Blouson dress.** Multicolor print on sand beige voile of polyester and cotton. Front-tucked bodice; buttons in back. $13 [$20-22] **Two-piece dress.** Polyester crepe with white lace bib of cotton and nylon. Blouse zips in back; skirt zips at side. $8 [$24-28]

Bottom row: Shirtwaist. White flower print on pink. polyester and rayon. Matching tie-belt; button-front. $7 [$15-18] **Shift.** Bright navy blue with white. Crepe of acetate and rayon bonded to acetate tricot for shape keeping. Back zipper. $8 [$18-20] **Two-piece outfit.** Bright orange Arnel® triacetate jersey dashed with white polka dots. Crisp white collar, button-back blouse, box-pleats skirt. $8 [$18-20] **A-line Dress.** Green and white print bodice rides low over green skirt. Rayon and silk with the look of linen. Back zipper. $11 [$20-22]

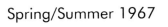

Top to bottom: Ribbed top sports turtleneck collar; cuffed raglan-style sleeves, elbow length. Back neck zipper. Cotton knit. $5 [$8-10] **A-line skirt** in flower printed cotton sailcloth. $4 [$12-15] **Subtly striped shirt,** lilac and pink, of imported Swiss cotton crinkle crepe. $7 [$8-10] **Kicky skirt** takes the A-line with four hip-stitched pleats in front. Crisp-textured rayon and flax. Matching-color vinyl belt. $6 [$12-15] **The Newsboy Cap.** Gold and orange print in rayon and cotton with a home-spun look. $3 [$15-18] **Sunshine-color shirt** of imported Swiss cotton crinkle crepe, double-yoke back with pleat, locker loop. $6 [$8-10] **Modified hip-rider skirt.** Bright orange and gold flower printed rayon and cotton with a homespun look. Belted contour waistline; side zipper. $5 [$20-24]

Whisp of a dress packs a beautiful wallop. Knit of Textralized® nylon yarn, it's so lightweight you hardly know it's there, yet it's un-crushable. Cowl collar; back zipper. $12 [$20-24] Shirred neckline on pullover style. $12 [$24-28] Pullover style with bateau neckline. $12 [$30-35] **Ball earrings** made of glass with gold-color metal ear-button and chain, clip back. $2 [$18-20]

Muscle shirt cut for active wear, all cotton mesh knit. $2 [$24-28] **Ringed crewneck.** 100 percent cotton. $2 [$20-22]

Derby wide rib. $1 [$12-15] **Flat knit** feels marvelously soft and resilient. $1.50 [$12-15] **Cotton crew neck** shirt. $2 [$12-15]

Top: Sweater shirt is knit to size. Ribbed placket, bottom and cuffs. Smart raglan shoulder styling. $6 [$15-18] **Cable design on chenille** texture sweater shirt. Looped-on rib knit long-point collar and placket. $6 [$40-45] **Sweater shirt** with two-tone rib knit front. Saddle shoulder styling. $9 [$40-45] **Lower left: Cool, comfortable cotton** mesh makes this sweater shirt the right choice for active sports as well as leisure wear. $5 [$20-25] **Mock-turtleneck** comes on strong as a springtime style favorite. Knit on narrow hemmed cuffs. Rib-knit bottom. $5 [$30-35] **Stripes and more stripes** make this a colorful knit sweater shirt. Roomy Dolman style sleeves. $4.92 [$18-20] **Lower right: Velvety velour in cotton knits.** Vertical stripe pullover, mock-turtleneck, solid-color ribbing across shoulders. $8 [$40-45]

Switch-around cotton wardrobe of floral prints and a knit top. Shift with rib-knit bodice. $6 [$8-10] Jacket with mock pockets. $5 [$20-22] A-line skirt. $5 [$12-15] Skinny-rib knit pullover; short sleeves. $4 [$8-10] Pants. $4 [$12-15] Jamaica shorts. $3 [$12-15]

Yellow, navy, and orange neon stripes with bright navy flash fashion. Jacket shaped with front and back seams. $10 [$15-18] Skirt goes A-line. Contour waist; back nylon zipper. $7 [$15-18] Striped Shell takes the diagonal line. Pullover style; cut-in shoulders; back neck nylon zipper. $5 [$12-15] Striped Pullover has stovepipe neck; back neck nylon zipper. $7 [$10-12] Pants in straight-leg style; elasticized waistband. $7 [$15-18] Striped Shift. Turtleneck; cut-in shoulders; back nylon zipper. $11 [$24-28] Wool felt cloche. Trimmed with rayon grosgrain band and bow. $6 [$18-20]

Striped turtleneck top, rib-knit. Back neck zipper. $4 [$10-12] Straight-leg pants. Narrow waistband and back zipper. Cotton corduroy. $5 [$15-18] Paisley print blouse. $4 [$12-15] Low-belted jumper zips in back. Cotton corduroy. $8 [$20-22] Jacket wears mock-pocket flaps. Cotton corduroy. $8 [$12-15] A-line skirt back zipper with button tab. Cotton corduroy. $5 [$12-15] Turtleneck Top. Gold cotton rib-knit. Back neck zipper. $4 [$10-12] The Cap. Visor style in cotton corduroy. $3 [$18-20]

Sporty pullover has turtleneck, turn-back cuffs, popcorn pattern and rib-stitching. $8 [$15-18] **Belted skirt** follows a modified A-line. Back zipper. $9 [$15-18] **Striped pullover** with crew-neck. $9 [$12-15] **Straight-leg pants.** Front slant pockets, adjustable tab inside waistband. Zipper fly-front. Rayon taffeta lined. $11 [$10-12]

Fall/Winter 1967

Lace cage of nylon over back-zippered crepe sheath of acetate and rayon. Special back interest: bowed, square neckline atop a pretty drift of soft gathers. $18 [$50-60] **Crepe skimmer** of acetate and rayon. Standaway collar, softly gathered front neckline. Back zipper. Lined with acetate taffeta. $15 [$40-45] **Princess costume** sheath and matching coat. Rayon and acetate woven with a lightly textured shantung-effect. Stand-up collar coat has acetate taffeta lining. Bare-arm sheath; jewel-neckline; back zipper. $11 [$40-45] **Swinger jewelry.** Austrian aurora crystal glass saucer beads. Ring is adjustable; fits all. Gold-color metal. $3 [$15-18] Drop earrings, clip-back. 2.25 inches long. $5 [$15-18]

Tent dress in a kaleidoscope print with solid-color tab and cuffs. Acrylic bonded to acetate tricot. $12 [$35-40] **Dandy skimmer** shows off ruffled bib and cuffs of white nylon and acetate lace. Bright red wool bonded to acetate tricot. $13 [$40-45] **Kiltie dress** with white low-waisted bodice; collar and short skirt in a woven plaid. Buckled-tab trim over side knife pleats. $15 [$45-50]

Three-piece outfit. Team the jacket with pants or skirt. $17.97 [$45-55] Jumbo-size checks. Jacket has mock-pocket flaps. Straight-leg pants zip in back. Slightly A-line skirt has contour waist, side zipper. **Two-piece costume.** Dress plays it solo or swings away with matching jacket. $23 [$55-60] Lively combo of deep gold-and-white tweed (wool worsted, acrylic, and rayon) and white jersey (wool and acrylic).

Sailor-girl dress looks spiffy in bright blue wool. $15 [$28-32] **Two-piece tunic dress** is military-minded with stand-up collar, buttons on the sleeves, crochet-look cotton knit bonded to acetate tricot. $11 [$35-40] **Pow-print dress** mixes pink and orange. Shift-shape ends in a flippy skirt. Wool bonded to acetate tricot. $15 [$35-40]

12

Cheers for checks, spirited two-piece dress. $11 [$40-45] **Military Airs** captured with chevron stripes, a line of buttons, all-around pleats. $10 [$35-40] **Outstanding** tent dress swings high, wide, and handsome from front-yoke. Twill of polyester and cotton. $9 [$35-40] **Lilting** knit-dress of polyester and cotton. $9 [$40-45]

A real-right solid-color and print combo. Over-blouse and skirt of polyester and cotton. Harmonizing-color print shirt of polyester, rayon, Bermuda collar. $11 [$45-50] **Pretty paisley** adds pow to the smock-dress. Spice brown multi-color printed poplin of rayon and cotton. $8 [$35-40]

Two-piece ensemble. Bright-buttoned acrylic coat has the look of wool. Knit dress has a long back zipper closing. $29 [$15-18] **Fedora hat.** Wool felt trimmed with rayon grosgrain band. $6 [$18-20] **Three-piece weekend set.** Jacket, skirt, and pants in a soft, nubby tweed of rayon, wool, and nylon bonded to acetate tricot for shape-retention and smooth appearance. $29 [$55-60 set]

Two-piece pleated dress. Wool jersey bonded to acetate tricot, over blouse has front button trim, button cuffs, long back zipper. Skirt is pleated from hip seam. $20 [$18-22] **Skimmer.** **Paisley-printed,** slightly textured wool bonded to acetate tricot. Two front-seam pockets. Long back zipper closing. $19 [$18-23] **Two-piece striped dress,** double-knit acrylic, turtleneck top, shiny moss green plastic belt. $22 [$40-45]

Rayon knit two-piece dress. Jacket has double-breasted effect; mock-pocket detail; snap-on rib-knit dickey. $13 [$30-35] Skimmer has tri-tone front and back panels, stand-up rolled collar; tie-bow trim. $11 [$24-28]

The mini-shift. Gold and black stripes whip around jersey, double-knit of triacetate and nylon. Cowl neck; back zipper; side slits. $9 [$35-45] The over blouse. Black and white screen print swirled on acetate surah. Shallow scoop neckline; back neck zipper. Trumpet-flared 3/4-length sleeves. $6 [$20-24] The Tunic. Inspired by and Indian rajah's costume. Cut long and slightly flared at hips. Mandarin collar, 3/4-length sleeves. $5 [$20-24] Casual hose. Stretch nylon mesh-knit. Seamless full-length. $2.85 [$NPA]

15

A square of Schiffli embroidery, an adaptation of the Mexican wedding blouse, in batiste of polyester and cotton. $6 [$20-22]
Bib front lavished with lace and pin tucks, batiste of polyester and cotton. Pullover, stand-up band collar. $6 [$20-22]

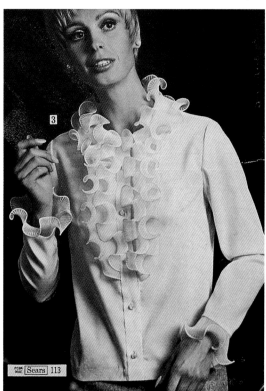

Our Dandy Blouse. Crepe and organza polyester. Ruffles lightly wired. Particularly notable with pant-suits or long, at-home skirts. $7 [$22-24]

Turtleneck pullover, wool knit, cuffed sleeves. $5 [$15-18]

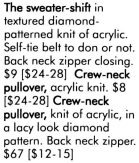

The sweater-shift in textured diamond-patterned knit of acrylic. Self-tie belt to don or not. Back neck zipper closing. $9 [$24-28] **Crew-neck pullover,** acrylic knit. $8 [$24-28] **Crew-neck pullover,** knit of acrylic, in a lacy look diamond pattern. Back neck zipper. $67 [$12-15]

Knits of 90 percent wool with 10 percent nylon for strength and shape-keeping. **Crew-neck pullover.** $5 [$12-15] **Crew-neck cardigan.** $6 [$12-15] **V-neck pullover.** $5 [$15-18] **Turtle-neck dickey.** Acrylic, a marvelous fill-in for all your V-neck sweaters. $2 [$4-6] **Bulky knit.** Warm cardigan with sporty wing collar, raglan sleeves, and covered buttons. $9 [$28-32]

Double-knit cotton dress, appliqué trim. $6 [$15-18] Knit dress in A-line style, smart white cowl collar. $6 [$15-18] A-line jumper with separate blouse, cotton knit. $8 [$12-15] Acrylic knit dress, drop-waistline flares into swinging skirt. $8 [$15-18] **Hat and bag set**, velveteen. $5 [$15-18]

GIRLS' SIZES

Some styles also in Chubby Girls' sizes

SWITCHEROO KNITS

Perma-Prest® coordinates of wrinkle-shy polyester and cotton. **Button-front shirt.** $4 [$8-10] **Swinging jumper.** $6 [$18-22] **Pleated skirt.** $5 [$10-12] **A-line skirt.** $4.75 [$10-12] **A-line shift.** $6 [$15-18] **Crew-neck pullover** of acrylic. $5 [$8-10] **Cardigan** of acrylic.

Crew-neck cardigan with flower design. $6 [$12-15] **Mock turtleneck pullover.** $4 [$8-10] **Pleated skirt.** Magic-grow feature, lengthened up to 1-1/2 inches. $6 [$12-15] **Squared-neck pullover** with short sleeves. $5 [$12-15] **A-line skirt,** double-knit hound's-tooth checks. $6 [$12-15] **Sweater dress,** pull-on. Turn-back cuffs. $9 [$20-22] **Bulky knit pullover,** brass color buttons trim left shoulder. $6 [$10-12] **Pants.** Double-knit, elastic waist. $6 [$8-10]

290 Sears PCBKM AEDSG

Sears 291

Color coordinated sweater and shirt sets of 100 percent virgin Orlon® acrylic. **Cable cardigan set,** sweater and contrasting shirt. $18 [$40-45] **Bold panel set** with full-cut sleeves. $15 [$45-50]

714 Sears PCDKM AEDSLG

Virgin wool traditionals. **Medium weight classic coat.** Worsted, two set-in pockets. Buttons and button holes sewn with nylon thread for added strength. Double elbows, reinforced seams. $7 [$35-40] **Classic zip coat,** worsted. Zipper front with rack-knit border. Set-in waist pockets, double elbows, reinforced neck and shoulder seams. $8 [$35-40] **Vest,** flat-knit with four sewn in pockets. $7 [$35-40]

Soft Cotton Velour Pullovers. **V-neck pullover.** $6 [$35-40] **Mock turtleneck.** Deep V contrast color insert. $6 [$35-40] Ban-Lon® sweater shirts of nylon. **Textured design,** diamond patterns and deep V design on front. Long point rib knit fashion collar. $8 [$45-50] **Full Fashioned Classic.** Knit to fit. Neat long raglan sleeves. $7 [$35-40] **Turtleneck** of combed cotton interlock knit with elastic in turn-down neck. Long sleeves. $3 [$18-20] **Acrylic dickeys.** $3 [$8-10]

Wool letter sweaters. **Award V-neck pullover,** worsted in baby shaker knit. $9 [$45-55] **Award cardigan.** Extra heavy and extra long two-ply wool worsted in baby shaker stitch. Button holes stitch with nylon thread for strength. $10 [$45-55]

Long gown in crepe of acetate and rayon. Square neckline, soft shirring, covered buttons accent bodice. A-line shaped skirt. $32 [$45-55] **Late-day dress** in crepe of acetate and rayon, V-neckline in front, acetate lining; A-shaped skirt. Attached cummerbund with bow. $35 [$40-45] **Late-day handbag** of black rayon faille, rayon satin lining. $9 [$25-30] **Late-day shoes.** Slinky and exciting, cross-strap styling at vamp. Softly squared toe and rayon *peau de soie* upper. 2-inch heel, elastic strap at back. $13 [$18-10]

Spring/Summer 1968

Dome ring, large simulated baroque pearl set in feather-like gold-color metal mounting. Adjustable. $5 [$10-12] **Chandelier earrings.** Jet-color Austrian aurora crystal glass beads, gold-color metal setting. $5 [$12-15] **Late-day stockings.** *Point d'esprit* pattern, seamless nylon in non-run knit. Nude. $1.50 [$NPA]

Note: A young woman on her way to the office would not have left the house without her shortie gloves for spring and summer. The same young lady would have worn her skirts short, but not more than three inches or so above her knees.

Skimmer dress with jacket in rayon and silk with the look of linen. Jacket is crisply outlined with white band and tabbed with mock pockets. $36 [$55-65 set] **Shoes** with patent vinyl uppers and gold-color metal buckle-trim. 1-5/8 inch heel. $13 [$18-20] **Chain-handle bag** of straw-look viscose rayon. $7 [$20-25]

Dress of woven checked cotton, comes with matching jacket with double-breasted effect. $38 [$35-40] **Hat** of synthetic straw, wide snap brim, tuck-away ribbon chin-ties. $10 [$20-25] **Handbag** of smooth vinyl. Inside zippered pocket. Rayon lining. $8 [$25-30] **Shoes** with calfskin uppers, high-rising tongue. 1-5/8 inch heel. $13 [$20-25]

Shift with funnel-shaped neckline; front yoke, chain belt of plastic imitates tortoise shell. Back zipper. $17 [$30-35]

22

Two-piece dress. Yoke top with back zipper has shoulder loops to hold acetate surah scarf. $12 [$30-35] **Skimmer dress** in a ribbed texture. Bright buttons trim front yoke. Back zipper. $13 [$30-35] **Three-piece dress.** Jacket and skirt with white blouse. $15 [$30-35] **Textured vinyl handbag.** Cotton print lining. Center zip pocket. About 10 x 7 x 4 inches. $5 [$25-30]

Shirt-look skimmer in rayon, cotton, and acetate. Button-and-placket trim. Back zipper. $10 [$25-30] **Shift with square neckline,** front yoke, roomy pockets, in rayon and acetate. Back zipper. $8 [$20-25] **Jacket-dress.** Jacket and skirt-portion of dress in woven checks of cotton and triacetate. Sleeveless bodice of dress in cotton broadcloth. $12 [$25-30]

Coat-skimmer in ottoman-ribbed fabric of cotton, acetate, and rayon. $10 [$20-25] **Dropped-waistline dress** of acetate jersey bonded to acetate tricot. Step-in style with front buttons, self belt. $10 [$20-25] **Halter-effect shift,** stand-up collar, rayon with the look of linen. Back zipper. $7 [$30-35] **Vanity box bag.** Smooth vinyl. Zip-pocket divider, rayon lined. $8 [$25-28]

24

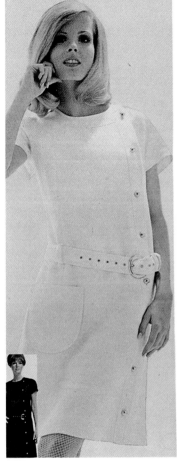

Coat-style dress in gabardine of rayon and acetate. Stitching accents its good lines. Gold-color metal buttons at side opening. Low-set belt; one patch pocket. $20 [$35-42] **Coat-dress** of ribbed, two-ply cotton, front seaming, mock-pocket flaps. $15 [$25-30] **Step-in skimmer** of rayon and acetate. Gold-color metal buttons, slanted mock-pocket tabs. $12 [$25-30]

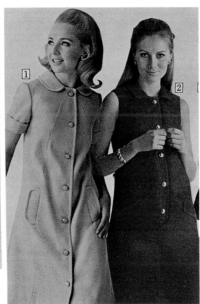

Modified tent dress. $12 [$35-40] **Shift of horizontal tucks,** front and back. Back zipper. $16 [$25-30] **Step-in shirt-shift** in floral flock-print. Cotton-lined. $14 [$20-25]

Peppy Pleats dress of polyester crepe. $13 [$25-30] Flower power bursts into print on crepe of polyester. Lined shift (except sleeves) has low neckline, zipper in back. $11 [$25-30] Tiers of tucks dress of rayon. $15 [$30-35] White dots on airy voile skimmer of polyester and cotton. $11 [$35-40] Frame handle bag. Shiny patent vinyl: rayon-lined. $8 [$20-28] Dashing sling. The shiniest of patent vinyls with smart squared-off toe and 1-3/4-inch blocky heel. $8 [$18-22]

Tie-front tweed coat and sleeveless skimmer of rayon, acetate, and silk. $25 [$40-42] Posy-print duo on polyester and cotton voile. Sleeveless dress has crisp rayon skirt, white cotton bodice, back zipper. $17 [$35-40] Jacket and dress in hound's-tooth checked cotton bonded to acetate tricot. Jacket has side loop and button closing, mock-pocket flaps. Sleeveless skimmer has back zipper. $18 [$20-25] Stripes 'n' solid partners in rayon and cotton canvas. Coat boldly striped in green and white is collar-less and belted high. Sleeveless skimmer is stark white with vertical striped inset band; back zipper. $15 [$35-40]

Note: Window-pane checks became an important design. The abstract line art of Piet Mondrian had a dramatic effect on late 1960s fashion, both in clothing and accessories.

Coat and dress of double-faced cotton fabric. Seam-pocketed coat. Sleeveless skimmer is belted low; zips in back. $19 [$40-45 set]

Pantdress and jumper, together or solo. Beige chino cloth jumper of polyester and cotton, pantdress in broadcloth of polyester and cotton. $16 [$45-50] **Knee-high boots.** Glossy stretch patent vinyl uppers, one-inch heel, about 16 inches high. $13 [$50-55]

Note: Knee-high boots gained in popularity. Appearing as a somewhat radical fashion statement in the mid-1960s, they were commonplace by 1968.

Print shift, wear with or without plastic link belt. Back zipper. $20 [$30-35]
Princess dress, front pleats; back zipper. $19 [$30-35] **Belted empire-style** dress; buttons in front. $20 [$30-35]

Opposite: Sleeveless **skimmer** dress, double-knit of textured acetate, jewel neckline; back zipper closing. $14 [$30-35] **Low-waist knit dress**, multicolor stripes. $13 [$25-30] Sleeveless sweater dress, acetate knit. Turtleneck; daisy pin; back zipper. $11 [$35-40] Pull-on style sweater dress knit of feather-light acrylic, basket-weave stitched yoke. $10 [$35-40]

Perky print of polyester and cotton, tucked front-bodice, belt with chain closing. $8 [$20-25] **Low pockets** atop twin-pleated yoked skimmer. Zips in back. Nubby-textured fabric of polyester and cotton. $9 [$30-35] **Woven windowpane plaid** of polyester and cotton treated with fabric protector. $9 [$25-30] **Costume dress** and mock-pocketed jacket. Cotton; dress zips in back. Hem can be lengthened. $13 [$30-35]

Left: Pantjumper. Windowpane checks woven of rayon and cotton. Bodice slants to a low-down waist. Back zipper. $10 [$25-30]

Right: A-line shift in straight stripes. Patch pocket; button trim; back zipper. Poplin of polyester and cotton. $8 [$28-30] **Pantshift with "dog collar"** and front zipper detailed with metal trim. Rib-textured polyester and cotton. $11 [$30-35] **Checked shift** with daisy pin. Back zipper. Twill of polyester and cotton. $9 [$28-30]

Striped shell with turtle-neck, polyester and nylon.
$5 [$15-18] **Short-sleeve top,** nylon. $5 [$15-18]
Jamaica shorts. $5 [$12-15] **pants.** $7 [$15-18]

T-shirt mini-shift. Pull-on style, scoop neckline, wear with or without chain belt for two great looks. Polyester and cotton knit. $8 [$20-24]
Dress and hat, combed cotton sateen; zips in back. $9 [$35-40 set]
Sleeveless shift skims to A-line. Wide belt is high; back zipper. Canvas cloth of rayon and cotton. $6 [$28-30] **Low-waist shift.** Cotton gingham, side-pleated skirt; back zipper. $7 [$30-32]

Double-knit and jersey go-togethers in mellow colors. **Sleeveless jacket** has yoke detail in front; closes with ball-buttons and loops. $9 [$15-18] **Slim skirt.** Narrow waistband; side zipper closing, length about 24 inches. $8 [$12-15] **Print shift** softly gathered, slit neckline, billowy sleeves, elasticized wrists; back zipper. $15 [$35-40] **Print shell** has a cowl collar; back neck nylon zipper. $6 [$15-18] **Straight-leg pants,** pull-on style. $10 [$20-22]

The polyester fiber in these coordinates is **FORTREL**

Go-togethers of rayon with the crisp look of linen. **Plaid shirt.** Pointed collar, button placket, button cuffs. $9 [$15-18] **Straight-leg pants** fully lined, back zipper. $9 [$20-22] **Sleeveless jacket,** gold-color metal link belt, mock-pocket flaps. $9 [$20-22] **Plaid pantskirt,** waistband; back zipper. $9 [$22-24] **Sleeveless shift,** dropped waist, gently gathered skirt, pockets in front skirt; back zipper. $13 [$25-30 set] **Sporty tote.** Cotton duck bag; patent vinyl trim. Zip-pocket. $5 [$20-25]

Note: Double knits of polyester were a fashion staple of the late 1960s. Women began to contemplate throwing away their irons and ironing boards. It was a new world!

"T-shirt" dress. Striped cotton knit; back zipper. $6 [$18-20] Pantdress of polka dot printed cotton poplin. Deep pleat in front and back for tent-shift shaping. Front zipper. $5 [$20-22]

Poplin shirtdress with button-down collar and barrel cuffs. $5 [$20-22] Jamaica shorts of oxford cloth, side zipper. $3.50 [$18-20]

Snappy poplin pantshift sports lowered waistline, step-in style, trimmed with cotton lace. $6 [$20-22] Puffed sleeve pull-over dress. Broadcloth with cotton lace trim. Back neck button. $5 [$20-22] Broadcloth over blouse has cotton lace trim and two pockets. $3 [$15-18] Poplin stovepipe pants have contour waist, back zipper. $5 [$15-18] Poplin Jamaica shorts with contour waist and back zipper. $3.59 [$15-18]

Pullover shirt, cotton knit, turtle appliqué. $3 [$8-10] **Knee pants.** Roll-up style in horizontal-stretch cotton duck. $3 [$20-22] **Walking shorts.** Smooth-fitting two-way stretch nylon knit has suede texture. $4 [$18-20] **Mini-culottes** in sharkskin of triacetate. Stitched pleat in front and back, side zipper. $6 [$12-15]

Left: Mix or match shift and pullover-tops knit of cotton; pants of double-knit cotton. **Striped shift.** A-line style with mini sleeves, zipper closing in back. $6 [$25-30] **Short-sleeve top** with jewel neckline; back zipper. $4 [$10-12] **Sleeveless shell** with mock-turtleneck; button closing at shoulder. $3 [$8-10] **Golf shirt** with button closing. $4 [$8-10] **Tank Top.** $3 [$12-15] **Straight-leg pants.** $6 [$18-20] **Walking shorts,** side zipper, button-tab closing. $4 [$12-15] **Short shorts** with back zipper, button-tab closing. $3 [$15-18]

Smooth, wrinkle-shy broadcloth fabrics retain their neat look. **Posy-printed shirt-shift** of rayon and cotton, button-down collar; patch pocket. $4.49 [$22-24] **Roll-sleeve shirt,** cotton, convertible collar; square bottom. $3 [$12-15] **Sleeveless shirt** in bright paisley print, cotton. $3 [$12-15] **Sleeveless shirt** has long tails, rayon and cotton, wild-flower print. $3 [$12-15] **Long-sleeve striped shirt** with a button-down collar, barrel cuffs, long shirt-tails. $4 [$10-12]

Sears 43

Tucked-front blouse has back-button closing, broadcloth of polyester and cotton. $4 [$10-12] **Crinkly-knit shell** of polyester, dropped back shoulder line; back neck zipper. $4 [$12-15] **Tank Top,** nylon knit. $4 [$18-20] **Straight-line skirt.** Matching vinyl belt. $5 [$15-18] **Sharkskin-look skirts** of triacetate with French waistband, side zipper. $6 [$12-15] **Straight-line skirt.** $6 [$12-15] **Novel shoulder bag.** Patent vinyl. $7 [$18-20]

34

Summer 1968

Skimmer with mock-pockets inspired by the popular safari look. Textured in a tiny waffle-weave, all-around yoke, back zipper closing. $10 [$35-40] **Shift** woven in a bird's eye pattern, mock-pocket flaps; front button trim, back zipper. $10 [$35-40] **Ribbing adds dimension** to this two-piece dress, high stand-up neckline; back zipper. A-line skirt zips at the side. $10 [$25-30]

Sleeveless skimmer prettied with acetate satin collar and tab trim. Cotton-and-nylon lace, fully lined with acetate; back zipper. $12 [$35-40] **Two-piece dress**, scalloped over blouse. Skirt has an elasticized waist. Acetate-and-nylon lace; lined with acetate. $12 [$35-40] **Sling pump** with vinyl upper, 1-5/8-inch heel. $6 [$20-22]

35

Skimmer, acetate and nylon knit in multi-color stripes. Step-in style with gold-color metal buttons. $11 [$30-35] Shift, narrow-striped double-knit acetate. Covered buttons trim front; back zipper. Tie belt. $11 [$30-35]

Cotton coat-shift with dainty lace trim, self belt included. $10 [$20-24] Broadcloth step-in style of polyester and rayon, dropped waistline, pleats. $10 [$20-24] Straw bag. Double-handle tote in summery natural-color straw accented with leather. $5 [$12-15]

36

Crepe of polyester. **Dropped-waistline dress** with a skirt of stay-in pleats, corded neckline; back zipper. $11 [$20-24] **Sleeveless shift.** Bow trim at one shoulder, diagonal yoke in front and back; back zipper. $11 [$30-35] **Saucy sandal.** Kidskin uppers, composition sole, 1-5/8-inch heel. $7 [$18-20]

Sleeveless skimmer with Bermuda-type collar, inverted front pleats, step-in style. $8 [$25-30] **Jaunty bi-color dress** with A-line skirt, dropped waist, rolled collar, two patch pockets. Two-tone self belt included; back zipper closing. $8 [$25-30] **Tote** in cotton duck. $6 [$12-15]

37

Skimmer dress in an abstract floral print. White bands at neck and hemline, half-belt buttons in back; back zipper. $8 [$25-30] **Culottes** in windowpane-check, dropped waist, stand-up collar, and front button-trim. $8 [$25-30]

38

Zip-front step-in dresses. **Printed cotton duck** accented with neat piping trim. Two pockets. $7 [$30-35] **Woven checked poplin** of rayon and acetate, reverse-check trims zipper opening, pockets. $7 [$30-35] **Solid-color cotton duck** with stand-up neckline; mock-pocket trim. $7 [$20-24]

Round sunglasses. Plastic optical frame; glass lenses. From Italy. $2 [$20-22] **Pant-dress** of cotton sateen, front zipper, stand-up collar, metal buckle on low-set belt. $7 [$35-40] **Culottes** of cotton duck, dropped-waist style, front and back over flap; back zipper. $7 [$25-30] **Sandal** has vamp straps connected by burnished metal rings, leather uppers, 1-1/4-inch heel. $5.90 [$18-20]

Full-skirted dress of polka-dot printed cotton percale. Buttons trim shoulders. $4 [$20-22] **Coat dress**, printed stripes on cotton percale. $4 [$20-22]

A-line step-in shift, paisley-printed cotton percale; self tie-belt included. $4 [$18-20] **Pullover dress** with scoop neckline and elasticized waist, cotton denim with white stitching; red and white belt and button trim, pocket. $4 [$18-20]

Shirtdress of woven checked cotton. $4 [$18-20] **Fly-front**, step-in shirtdress with concealed zipper. Woven striped seer-sucker of acetate and cotton. $4 [$18-20]

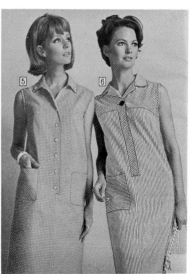

Perma-Prest® fashions in challis of rayon and polyester. **Step-in style** in printed stripes with button-down collar, front button placket, one pocket. Mother's. $6 [$20-24] Big Sister's. $5 [$15-18] Little Sister's. $4 [$12-15] **Pant-dress.** Front-zippered step-in style, printed checks. Mother's. $6 [$20-24] Big Sister's. $5 [$15-18] Little Sister's. $4 [$12-15]

40

The new "body" shirtdress. Button-front; high pointed collar. Green and white striped cotton duck. $8 [$24-28] Flower power, combed cotton sateen, buttons all the way down. $8 [$28-32]

Summer 1968

From left, clockwise: **Pants Set.** Ribbed polyester and cotton. $8 [$24-28] **Pant playdress.** Daisies on front yoke, duck of cotton and rayon, zips in back. $7 [$20-24] **Sun hat.** Squared-off brim on sectioned crown, cotton sailcloth. $2.39 [$12-15] **Pantdress** goes nautical with ribbed polyester and cotton. $8 [$30-35] **Shorts take cover** under mini-tunic of white cotton brocade. $9 [$30-35] **Sandal sparkle.** Simulated colored stones, leather. $6.90 [$22-24] **Pantdress** with over-skirt to show off attached white pants. $8 [$20-24] **Short-stop pantdress** and a rope of white beads. Cotton poplin. $8 [$20-24]

Spun-bonded polyester for smart style, low price. **Pop dots** liven tie-shoulder style, ties of bias tape for smooth fit. $2 [$15-18] **Enticing scoop neckline** swoops to a low V in back, finished with a bow. $2 [$18-20] **Stand-up band collar** gives way to soft tucks over bustline. Cut-out shoulders. Oriental flower design in stripe. $2 [$15-18] **Loose, swingy tent dress** for summer fun and frolic. Ties at back neckline. $2 [$18-20]

Note: Shifts were available in every combination of color and bold floral prints. Polyester was the fabric of choice for easy washing without wrinkling. These colorful prints are popular with collectors who wear them as beach cover-ups and summer dresses.

Cool style to make the summer scene. Smooth-fitting yoke, ruffle sleeve, patch pocket, back hook. $3 [$18-20] **A column of a dress** with cutaway armholes for an elegant bare-shoulder look. Sash to tie under bust or at waist. $3 [$20-24] **Wide scoop neckline** edged with large ruffle for the heralded romantic look. Can be worn off the shoulder. $3 [$15-18] **Go everywhere dress.** Sleeve with soft elasticized ruffle, back tie. $3 [$18-20]

Modified A-liner in poplin of rayon and polyester, front zipper and pockets. $6.50 [$12-15] Flower-power shift in poplin of rayon and cotton, back zipper closing. $6.50 [$12-15] Culottes-shift in a challis of rayon and polyester, plastic belt, back zipper. $6.50 [$18-20] Striped cotton poplin with sailor-inspired collar, back zipper closing. $6.50 [$12-15] Gingham dress of polyester and cotton, button-down collar, button front. $6.50 [$12-15]

The shift, to wear belted or not. Back zipper. $15.95 [$40-45] Skimmer with front yoke, removable bow. $14 [$40-45] Skimmer with "V" yoke, inverted front pleat, back zipper. $15 [$40-45]

Fall/Winter 1968

43

Shift with long pointed sleeves, acetate and nylon lace, lined, except sleeves, with acetate tricot; back zipper. $14 [$45-50]
Shift with ruffled collar and cuffs, lace of acetate, nylon and rayon, satin bow. $15.95 [$45-50]
Jewelry. Rhinestones, beautifully mounted in metal. Hinged bangle-bracelet. $5 [$25-30] Wedding-band style earrings, clip back. $3 [$15-18] Dome ring, 3/4-inch wide, adjusts. $2 [$15-18]

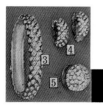

Coat and dress ensemble of shimmery acetate that looks like silk. Striped coat has matchbox seams curving close; double-breasted closing; fully lined. Opens up to show A-line skimmer with scoop neckline and tiny shoulder straps; back zipper. $25 [$50-55] **Medieval charmer.** Jacket, skirt, and pants trio in rayon and cotton faille. Fencer jacket cropped short; highlighted with glitter buttons; stand-up collar. Dirndl skirt and straight-leg pants have high-rise band and back zipper. $19 [$85-95]

A-line skimmer of acetate and rayon crepe with satin trim. Neckline is low-squared in back, scooped in front. Back zipper. $15 [$50-55] Nostalgic lace dress of cotton, acetate, and rayon. Ruffled scoop neckline. Dirndl skirt cinched with rhinestone-buckled acetate satin belt, taffeta lined; back zipper. $20 [$50-55] Perma-Prest® dress of polyester rib-knit, cowl-collar, short sleeves. $18 [$50-55] Victorian look in mini or midi-length dress. Lace bodice. Ruffle and button trimmed, dirndl skirt of black cotton velveteen, tie-back sash, back zipper. $18 [$40-45]

Textured hosiery sold on page 407

The Young Romantics

Body blouses in crepe of triacetate. Poet collar with beguiling sleeves, French cuffs. $45 [$12-15] **Ruffled front** and cuffs. $6 [$18-20] **Pleated ruffles** around ascot flip-tie, deep barrel-cuffs. $6 [$18-20]

Body sweater knit of acrylic, deep turtleneck; back neck zipper. $7 [$10-12] **Bow-tie blouse** of broadcloth polyester and cotton, button barrel-cuffs. $5 [$8-10] **High-rise front jumper** skims to the A-line. Woven acrylic plaid bonded to acetate tricot. Jewel-neckline jumper; front-tabbed; back-zippered. $11 [$35-40] **Fitted and flared** wool flannel bonded to acetate tricot. Scoop-neckline jumper; front center welt seam and swingy pleat; back zipper. $12 [$35-40] **Low-waisted** and A-shaped jumper teams up solid-color 'n' plaid. Nylon-and-rayon fabrics bonded to acetate tricot, jewel neckline; flap trim; back zipper. $13 [$35-40]

Lace coat of cotton and nylon has a hook closing at the neckline. Matching lace overlays top of dress in front and back, crepe dress of acetate and rayon; back zipper closing; 2-inch hem. $26 [$55-65]

Floor-length lace dress of acetate and nylon; acetate lined. Front and back panels of organza fall from a yoke band of satin with front bow; back zipper. $25 [$40-45] **Crepe dress** of acetate and rayon. Midriff section of cotton lace. Floor and street lengths. $21 [$45-50] **Empire dress**, rayon chiffon fall free from the shoulders in back, satin band and bow; back zipper. $23 [$35-40]

Sleeveless dress of ribbed rayon and acetate. White vinyl belt and buttons. $14 [$35-40] Coachman style, rayon with the look of linen. White piping and buttons, two-seam pockets. $19 [$40-45] V-neck dress in woven plaid of rayon and acetate with detachable white dickey of ribbed rayon and acetate. $15 [$35-40]

Culottes-shift with its own skirt, white cotton canvas with a pastel posy print. Culottes-shift closes with ball-buttons. Back-wrap dirndl skirt ties at waist, has a pair of patch pockets. $11 [$30-35] Farmer-girl culottes in cotton canvas. Equipped with flap-top patch pockets; side zipper. Straps and bib-front button off. $9 [$35-40]

232 Sears

Nehru-look mini-mate set. Cotton pique, screen-print trim, back zipper. Pull-on shorts. $8 [$40-45] **Mini-mate set.** Cotton with a sprinkling of green clip-dot flowers. Daisy chains rim modified square neckline, puffy sleeves, and ruffled legs. Pull-on bloomer-shorts. $9 [$35-40] **Country-girl culottes-shift** of cotton and rayon; stand-up collar, mock suspenders, back zipper. $7 [$35-40] **Culottes-shift** in white cotton canvas with square neck, flap-panel in front and back, culottes legs underneath, back zipper. $7 [$25-30]

Soft box-plaid suit, blend of wool, rayon, and nylon, braid-outlined, bracelet-length sleeves; skirt zips at side. $35 [$55-65]

Bright dash of jacket, precisely seamed front and back; and two-tone sleeveless dress that flares to A-shape; zips in back. Crisp rayon with the look of linen. $18 [$40-45] **Polka dot** shirt-and-skirt look has crepe bodice of polyester and triacetate. $15 [$40-45] **Awning stripes** on super-long jacket cover a white sleeveless dress with low-swinging pleats; back zipper. Cotton canvas. $15 [$40-45] **Color comes on happy** in a long boy-jacket and sleeveless A-line skimmer with modified scoop-neck, back zipper closing. Rayon and silk look like linen. $14 [$40-45]

Mock turtle-
neck shirt in
super-soft
acrylic. $8
[$18-20]
Perma-Prest®
cotton slacks.
$8 [$18-20]

Striped knit shirt of easy-care
Orlon®. $11 [$18-20]

Cardigan of 50 percent virgin alpaca, 50 percent virgin wool, color-matched buttons. $16 [$20-24] **Orlon® sweater shirt** knit in an airy, open stitch acrylic. $8 [$20-24] **Sears Best crew socks**, 75 percent soft, spun, high bulk acrylic and 25 percent stretch nylon. $1.35 [$NPA]

Playsuit set for grown-up girls, seersucker of triacetate and cotton. Button-front pantshift is elasticized at waist. Dirndl skirt has front buttons, side pocket. $9 [$30-35] **Patriotic pantshift** in duck of rayon and cotton. Front zipper. Removable tie. $8 [$45-50]

The HANDBAG
Safari-look tote in patent vinyl. Large outside front pocket. Welting trim. Unlined. About 12½x8x4 in.
88 J 2193–Bone beige
88 J 2194–White
88 J 2195–Black
Wt. 2 lbs. 10 oz.
Each......$5.99

Peppy pantshift with ball-buttons, tie belt; of rayon/cotton sailcloth. $7 [$45-50] Culottes-shift, safari-style, in cotton chambray. Button closing; button-trimmed pockets. Stitched-down front pleat; belt. $8 [$45-50] Bra-pantshift in a twill of cotton and rayon. Front pockets; back nylon zipper. Adjustable shoulder straps; bra closure is independent of the shift. $9 [$45-50] Mini-mates set with pullover shift and pull-on shorts in poplin of rayon and cotton. $7 [$40-45] Tote bag in cotton duck. $7 [$12-15]

Two-piece dress in waffle-effect knit of triacetate and nylon. Notch-collared jacket has mock-pocket trim. Skirt has elasticized waist; 2-inch hem. $10 [$25-30] Front-pleated skimmer. Thick-and-thin ottoman ribbed effect knit of acetate and nylon. Back zipper; 2-inch hem. $10 [$25-30]

Note: Pantdresses and mini-shifts were popular for young girls as well as women. Most of the fabrics required little or no ironing.

A-line shift with button-front panel prettily edged in daisies. $4.50 [$24-28] **Mini-mates** set, shifty-top has daisy trim; back buttons. Cotton duck shorts; elasticized waistband. $5 [$24-28] **Swimsuit.** Scooped neck top, daisy trim. Pull-on pants. $4.50 [$30-35] **Pantdress** with daisy trim. $5 [$24-28]

Dropped waistline dress falls to an A-line. Rolled collar ends with a flippy tie. Back zipper. 2-inch hem. $9 [$25-30]
Band-collared skimmer. Button-trimmed tabs top the softly pleated sides. Back zipper. 2-inch hem. $10 [$25-30]

54   Summer 1969

Jacquard-patterned wool knit sweaters. Pullover style with double fabric mock turtleneck collar. His $16 [$40-45] Hers $16 [$35-40]

Suede and textured knit add a new dimension to classically styled sweaters for men. **Brown cardigan** of 100 percent virgin wool, front jacquard panel, suede covered buttons. $19 [$50-55] **Gold cardigan.** Stitched suede panels with acrylic ottoman knit. Suede covered buttons. $22.50 [$50-55] **Green pullover** of virgin wool. Front jacquard panel, double-fabric rib knit mock-turtle collar, cuffs, buttons. $18 [$50-55]

A-line style has two slot-seam pockets, non-roll French waistband. $10 [$12-15] **Straight-line style** has non-roll French waistband. $9 [$15-18] **Side-pleated style** has a band-less waistline, tab and button trim. $10 [$15-18]

A-line classic jumper in wool flannel bonded to acetate tricot. Front welt seams; back nylon zipper. $10 [$20-24] **Belted A-line jumper** in a woven glen plaid of wool, nylon, and mohair. Self belt buttons in front. Mock pockets; back zipper. $14 [$20-24] **Princess-style jumper** in acrylic double-knit, V-neckline; shiny buttons; patch pocket. $13 [$20-24] **Pullover** of stretch nylon knit with turtle-neck and back-neck zipper. $5 [$8-10] **Scarf** of silk twill with hand-rolled edges. $3.50 [$15-18]

Note: By the fall of 1969, the mini skirt was about as short as it would ever get.

Navy jumper has U-neckline, front and back; pullover style. Mock turtleneck sweater knit of acrylic. $22 [$40-45] **Sweater dress** with Tyrolean-effect bands around jewel-neckline, high-pocket, knit of wool-and-mohair. Short sleeves; modified A-line style zips in back. $17 [$30-35] **Vested step-in dress** has crepe shirt-style bodice of triacetate; cotton knit skirt, modified A-line style; cross-over belt. $18 [$40-45] **Shirtdress** has step-in entry via two-button tab-front. Turtle emblem; button cuffs; tie-belt to wear or not. Double-knit polyester. $17 [$30-35]

Plaid and solid in a wrap dress of acetate and nylon bonded to acetate tricot for shape-keeping. $13 [$30-35] **Jumper and shift.** Camel tan wrap-jumper of acetate and nylon (looks like wool basket weave) bonded to acetate tricot. Jabot shift of rayon and cotton; back zipper. $14 [$30-35] **High-spirited dress** in a plaid woven of acetate and nylon bonded to acetate tricot. Rayon and linen collars and cuffs. $12 [$30-35] **Natty vest** over navy and white dress. Acrylic knit vest and A-line skirt, low-waisted bodice of textured cotton and polyester; detachable tie. $15 [$30-35]

Print shift in oxford cloth of polyester and cotton. Front yoke; back zipper. $9 [$20-24] **Tucked, button-front dress** in poplin of polyester and cotton. $11 [$24-28] **Dress with wide collar**, low-waisted bodice, front-pleated skirt, vinyl belt. Woven plaid of polyester and cotton. $10 [$20-24]

Blouse with ruffles down the front and around the cuffs. Button-front, triacetate crepe. $6 [$12-15] **Suspender hang-up** with hi-rise waistband, front pleats, suspenders button off. Back zipper. $10 [$24-28] **Ribbed turtleneck** pullover knit of acrylic. Back neck zipper. $7 [$8-10] **Button-front jumper,** flap-trim. Textured wool bonded to acetate tricot. $13 [$20-24] **Plaid jumper,** hip-banded low with side-swinging pleats, jewel neckline. Back zipper closing. $12 [$24-28]

Left three: Swingy dress with pop-art flowers on poplin of polyester and cotton. White ruffled collar and cuffs. Back zipper. $10 [$20-24] **Wrap dress** buttons high. White stitching and trim. Poplin of polyester and cotton. $11 [$24-28] **Dress in woven plaid** of polyester and cotton. Big jabot, long sleeves with eyelet embroidered ruffles. Low pleats. Back zipper. $11 [$24-28]

59

Chapter Two

Pants, Pantjumpers, Pantskirts, and Tunics

Hip-rider pants cinched with wide vinyl belt, metal-buckled. Band-less top; zipper fly-front. $6 [$20-24] **Sailcloth** with gold and orange print on yellow. $5 [$15-18] **Denim.** $4 [$15-18] Top partners. **Sizzle-stripe pull-on.** Cotton rib-knit. $3 [$12-15] **Lean, lanky pullover** has "jelly bean" sleeves. Combed cotton rib-knit. $3 [$12-15] **Ranch-style shirt** of checked polyester and cotton. Epaulets; banded collar; double-yoke back. $5 [$8-10]

JUNIOR BAZAAR

Turtleneck top. Wear neck-zipper in front or back. Cotton knit. $2.90 [$8-10] **Nattily checked pants** in hip-rider style; band-less waist; vinyl belt; stovepipe legs. Cotton. $7 [$20-24] **Dapper dot shirt** sports pointy collar, necktie detaches. Cotton print. $5 [$18-20] **Mod-ish jeans** with contrast stitching on hip-riding garrison waist, bellows-pockets. Straight-legs; zipper fly-front, snap closure. Cotton duck. $5 [$12-15] **On-parade jacket** has epaulets; a march of military buttons; welt pockets. Cotton duck. $7 [$20-22] **Dandy pin-striped pants** ride low on the hips, band-less waist with red slicker belt, stovepipe legs; zipper fly-front, cotton sailcloth. $6 [$18-20] **Visor Cap.** $3 [$15-18]

40 Sears

Sears 41

Pink top with square-neck; set-in sleeves. Cotton rib-knit. $4 [$8-10] **A-line skirt** with self-fabric belt; back zipper. Polyester and cotton sailcloth. $7 [$12-15] **Roman-striped top,** pullover-style, square-neck; raglan-style sleeves. Cotton rib-knit. $4 [$8-10] **Pink stovepipe pants**; back zipper. Polyester and cotton sailcloth. $7 [$18-20] **Yellow pullover** with scoop-neckline. Cotton rib-knit. $4 [$8-10] **Striped pants** in straight-leg style; contour belt, bandless waist; zipper fly-front. Polyester and cotton sailcloth. $8 [$20-24] **Striped shell** in scoop-neck pullover style. Cotton rib-knit. $4 [$8-10] **Violet Jamaicas,** bandless top; back zipper. Polyester and cotton sailcloth. $4 [$12-15]

Pedal pushers with adjustable waist; side zipper, saddle stitching, two front pockets. Cotton. **Denim.** Narrow loops; cuffed legs. $2.50 [$24-28] **Twill.** Tunnel loops; side leg slits. $3.50 [$24-28] **Classic jeans** with concealed side zipper; twill of sturdy cotton or denim. $3 [$45-50] **Perma-Prest® shirt** in woven checks of polyester and cotton. $4 [$12-15]

Pea jacket, flat-knit windowpane plaid bonded to acetate tricot to retain shape. $9 [$20-22] Matching straight-leg pants. Side zipper. $6 [$12-15] Square-neck pullover. $3 [$8-10] Walking shorts. $4 [$12-15] Shift with solid-color rib-knit bodice, flat-knit plaid skirt. Back-neck zipper. $8 [$20-24] Rib-knit pullover. Back-neck zipper. $3 [$8-10] Hip-rider shorts. Back zipper. Vinyl belt. $5 [$20-22] Dutch-boy cap of heavy cotton duck. $2.67 [$18-20]

Tank top. $5 [$8-10] Shirt with button-down collar, placket-front; long, button-cuffed sleeves. $7 [$8-10] Short shorts. $5 [$20-22] Bermuda shorts. $5 [$18-20] Princess-style jacket. $9 [$20-22] A-line skirt. $5 [$12-15] Bell-bottom pants. Contour vinyl belt, back zipper. $6 [$40-45] Folding flatties with cotton hopsacking uppers; Ribbon laces. $3.50 [$40-45]

Striped pullover, acrylic knit. $8 [$12-15] Ginger pants, wool flannel, straight-legs; narrow waistband. $9 [$18-20] Ginger pullover outlined with black, acrylic knit. $6 [$12-15] Checked skirt. Wool and nylon bonded to acetate tricot. Modified A-line; side zip; belt. $9 [$18-20]

Plaid jacket. Mock pockets; back vents; lined. $18 [$18-20] Plaid pants, straight-leg style. Contour waist; back zipper. Lined. $11 [$18-20]

Cardigan sweater. Wool knit, rib-knit trim. $11 [$15-18] Plaid A-line skirt. Contour-waist, buckle-belt. Back zipper. $10 [$18-20] Long sleeve sweater of wool-knit, pullover style; self belt. $11 [$18-20] Plaid wraparound kilt. $11 [$18-20]

Ginger jacket of wool flannel bonded to acetate tricot. Flap trim. $13 18-20] Matching checked pantskirt. $10 [$24-28] Dotted shirt of cotton oxford cloth. $5 [$18-20] Ginger skirt, wool flannel. Hip-stitched pleats, contour waist; buckle-belt; side zipper. $9 [$12-15]

Note: Low-riding pants are most interesting to collectors. Many of these styles had wide belts. Almost all had front zippers, which were not used in women's pants until the 1960s.

Military-look pants in cotton-and-nylon stretch denim. Welt-seamed waistband; straight-legs. Zipper fly-front; tab, button closing. $5 [$20-24] **Low-riding pants** feature a wide belt, crescent pockets, straight-legs. Ribbed twill of polyester/cotton. $8 [$24-28] **Tattersall pants** in woven checks of polyester and cotton. $6 [$24-28] **Shirt** with button-down collar; double-yoke in back; barrel cuffs, polyester and cotton. $4 [$10-12] **Multi-striped top** with stovepipe neckline, back neck zipper. Cotton knit. $4 [$12-15] **Knit shell** in stretch nylon. Mock turtleneck; back neck zipper closing. $3 [$10-12]

Oxford cloth jumper goes A-line. Front yoke; back zipper. $9 [$30-35] **Striped pullover.** Back neck zipper. Cotton knit. $4 [$15-18] **Oxford cloth pants.** Narrow waistband, fly-front, zipper closing. $7 [$15-18]

Spring/Summer 1968

Above: Collared top edged with scallops. Buttons in back. $4 [$15-18]
Jamaica shorts. Back zipper. $5 [$18-22] **Scoop-neck top,** scallop outlined,
bias tab in front. Button back. $4 [$15-18] **Pants.** Band-less top; back zipper.
$6 [$18-20] **Boy jacket** sports rounded collar. $8 [$18-20] **Skirt.** Band-less top,
back zipper. $6 [$15-18] **Shift.** Standaway band collar; scallop trim. Back
zipper. $9 [$24-28]

Right: Pants: Revved-up check pants of woven hound's-tooth polyester and
combed cotton. Disc-and-metal-ring belt. Back zipper. $6 [$24-28] **Polyester
and cotton** woven with a home-spun texture, welt-seamed contour waist;
buttonhole pockets. $6 [$22-24] **Twin Seaman, First Class** cotton duck pants.
$5 [$24-28] Tops: **Racing Checks** score high. Mini shirt ties to show off your
midriff. Banded button-down collar; button barrel cuffs. Cotton print. $4 [$24-
28] **Twin Stripes rim** white cotton knit pullover. Muscle sleeves. $4 [$12-15]
Pinstripes run about cotton knit pullover. $3 [$12-15] **Cotton duck mini bag.**
Shoulder strap detaches to wear as belt. $5 [$20-24]

Spring/Summer 1968

Note: *Stretch pants came into fashion in the mid- to late-1960s. Made of double-knit nylon, these pants kept their shape, and could be machine washed and needed little or no ironing. Styles have changed, but the basic concept hasn't for thirty years. Collectors are most interested in the flared leg and bell-bottom styles.*

Pull-on style double-knit nylon stretch pants, elasticized waistband; stitched creases. $8 [$18-22] **Multicolor** print pullover of nylon, Bateau-neck. $9 [$18-20]

Proportioned pants of double-knit nylon with two-way stretch. Pull-on; stitched creases. $11 [$18-22] **Vertical-stretch gabardine** pants of polyester and cotton. Contour stirrups. $6 [$18-22] **Perma-Prest®** pants in vertical-stretch shantung of rayon and nylon. Side-leg slits. Nylon side zipper. $9 [$18-22] **Bateau-neck pullover** in nylon. Wear tucked in or out. $4 [$12-15] **Sleek double-knit acetate** shirt in a bright screen print. Cowl collar; back neck zipper closing. Side vents. $9 [$20-22]

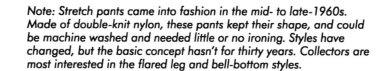

CPBK MAE Sears 85

Pantshift with back zipper, polyester/cotton knit. $9 [$35-40] **Flowery culottes-shift** printed broadcloth of cotton/rayon. Button-front; button-down collar. $7 [$25-30] **Nautical culottes-shift** with sailor collar; navy trim and tie. Zips in back. Cotton twill. $7 [$30-35]

HEY, MOM... PUT ON **YOUR** PLAYCLOTHES AND **C'MON** OUT!

Sears 29

Bright yellow jumpsuit, tidy V-neck, button-front closing, step-in style, double-knit cotton. $9 [$25-30] **Mini-mates** of cotton duck, button-down collar, button-front placket opening, shirt-tail bottom. Shorts have back zipper. $8 [$30-35] **Gingham duo** of cotton. Top has puffy, elasticized sleeves; bow, and back neck zipper. Dirndl-style culottes has self-belt, side zipper. $10 [$30-35]

Tapered-leg pants with leg vents; back zipper. $4.50 [$18-20] Culottes with a wrap-effect front panel, back action pleat; side zipper, button closing. $6 [$12-15] Tank top in white with bold print design on front. $3.50 [$20-22] Natty top, striped, back neck zipper. $3.50 [$15-18] Folding flatties. Patent vinyl upper; composition sole and heel. $4 [$12-15]

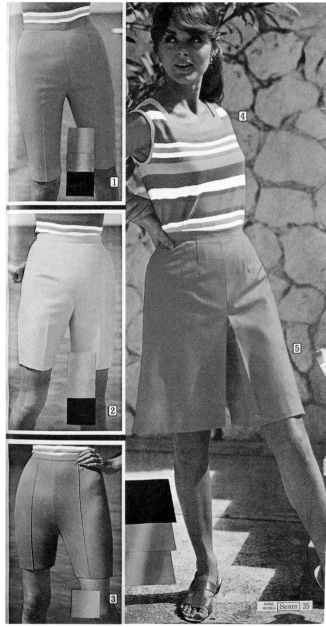

Team-up pullover in horizontal stripes knit of Monsanto Blue polyester and cotton. $4 [$15-18] Poplin A-line culottes of polyester and cotton, action-pleat front and back; narrow waistband; side zipper. $5 [$12-15]

"GEE, MOM...GUESS **I** NEED A COVER-UP!"

Summer's newest set. Shirt-style romper goes on its own or covers up with a color-cued wrap-skirt. Color-cued wrap-skirt in bone beige cotton sateen has side pleat, yoke front, side button closing, vinyl belt. $10 [$45-50]

Striped knit pullover. $3 [$8-10] **Pants,** cotton-lined. Tapered-leg style; side zipper. $5 [$12-15] **Knit shell.** Back neck zipper. $3 [$8-10] **Print Jamaicas,** cotton-lined. Side zipper. $3.44 [$10-12] **Sleeveless shirt,** wear in or out. Bermuda collar. $3 [$8-10] **Skirt,** cotton-lined, side zipper; hemp belt. $5 [$10-12] **Print shirt,** banded Hoover collar. Straight bottom. $3 [$8-10] **Jamaica shorts,** cotton-lined. Side zipper closing. $3 [$10-12]

Print blouse, stand-up collar, lace trim. $6 [$10-12] White pants, straight-legs, back zipper. $6 [$12-15] Print scoop-neck top, lace trimmed tab, button-back. $4 [$8-10] White Jamaica shorts. $5 [$12-15] Print dress. Empire bodice, back zipper. $9 [$20-24] Print bra. $2.50 [$12-15] Print mini-pettislip. Lace trimmed. $3 [$12-15] Print panty. $1.50 [$NPA] Sun hat with wide ripple-brim. $40 [$15-18]

Hi-voltage duo in double-knit cotton. Pullover tank top, Jamaica shorts. $6 [$12-15 set] Stretch denim Jamaica shorts, woven tattersall checks, cotton and nylon. $4 [$20-24] Cotton denim Western Jamaicas. Hip-rider style, vinyl belt. $4 [$20-24] Checked culottes skirt, front and back pleats, woven checks of cotton/triacetate. $5 [$10-12] Flag striped Jamaica shorts, cotton sailcloth. $4 [$18-20]

Pull-on tank top knit of polyester/cotton. $3 [$8-10] **Floral-print Jamaica shorts** in polyester and cotton that looks like homespun. $4 [$12-15] **Knit shell,** art nouveau screen print on bouclé-textured stretch nylon. Back neck zipper. $4 [$12-15] **Jamaica Shorts** in sailcloth of polyester and cotton. $4 [$12-15]

Summer coordinates of woven striped cotton seersucker frosted with white ruffles of embroidered cotton eyelet. **Butterfly crop top** buttons in back. $3 [$15-18] **Short shorts.** $2 [$8-10] **Over blouse,** back button closing. $3 [$8-10] **Jamaica shorts,** back zipper. $3 [$8-10] **Middy dress,** back zipper. $4 [$15-18] **Pantshift** buttons in front. $4 [$18-20]

Summer 1968

A-line skirt. $4 [$8-10] **Tailored Jamaica shorts.** $3 [$8-10] **A-line skimmer dress.** $5 [$18-20] **Blouse,** polyester/cotton broadcloth, Bermuda collar. $3 [$8-10] **Pantdress** features front ring-pull zipper and white cotton collar. $4 [$18-20] **Crop top.** $2 [$12-15] **Tapered pants,** back zipper. $3.50 [$8-10] **Jamaica shorts,** back zipper. $3 [$8-10] **Pullover** of cotton and polyester knit. $3 [$8-10]

Bouclé turtleneck pullover. $10 [$10-12] **Double-knit skirt.** $9 [$10-12] **Bouclé screen-print** pullover. $10 [$18-20] **Double-knit pants.** $11 [$18-20] **Bouclé V-neck** cardigan. $11 [$12-15] **Bouclé slim skirt.** $9 [$12-15] **Bouclé shell.** $8 [$10-12]

Pullover sweaters blend lamb's wool, nylon, and rabbit hair. Color-coordinated pants and skirts are tailored of wool flannel bonded to acetate tricot.
Jewel-neck sweater. $6 [$15-18] **Modified A-line skirt.** $6 [$15-18] **V-neck sweater.** $7 [$18-20] **Straight-leg pants.** $7 [$18-20]

73

Tunic and pants. Outfit in black crepe with white printed pinstripes. Acetate and rayon bonded to acetate tricot. Back zipper. $20 [$65-75] **Shoes** with black patent leather upper, closed back, cut-out sides. $9 [$40-45] **Double oval drop earrings,** clip-back. $3 [$8-10] **Bold-link bracelet watch,** box-clasp closing. $17 [$15-18]

Sleeveless pullover of textured stretch nylon knit. Jewel neckline; back neck zipper. $6 [$20-24] **Double-knit walking shorts** of nylon. $5 [$12-15] **Long-sleeved turtleneck pullover** of nylon; back neck zipper. $4 [$8-10] **Twill-weave walking shorts** of rayon and nylon. $6 [$12-15]

Walking shorts of double-knit polyester. $7 [$12-15] **Print pant top** in nylon jersey, bateau neckline. $5 [$18-20]

Turtleneck tunic, A-shaped style goes with or without its own tie-belt. Back nylon zipper closing. $7 [$35-40] **Dot top** copies the look of a weave. Turtleneck style with back-neck nylon zipper. $4 [$8-10] **Tank top**, stripes, scoop neckline. $3 [$10-12] **"T" top,** short-sleeved, ribbed trim at crew neck. $4 [$8-10] **Short shorts** with elasticized waistband. $3 [$12-15] **Walking shorts** with front creases. $4 [$10-12] **Flare-leg pants** complete with cuffs, elasticized waistband. $7 [$25-30]

Wrap shift ties with a tasseled belt. Hidden snaps at neckline, waistline. $10 [$24-28] **Voile Shirt** of polyester and cotton. Lined, except sleeves. $7 [$20-24] **Shaped skirt,** all-around yoke, side shirring, seam pockets, and back zipper. $7 [$12-15] **Pocketed vest.** $7 [$18-20]

Tank-top pullover in tulip-design print, nylon knit. $6 [$12-15] **Jewel-neck pullover** in a brush-stroke multicolor print of polyester knit. Back neck zipper closing. $6 [$12-15] **Stretch shots,** double-knit nylon, elasticized waistband. $5 [$10-12] **Shorts** in double-knit polyester with a twill-look, elastic waistband. $6 [$10-12]

Flared-leg pants, fly-front zipper. $7 [$25-30] **Bush shirt** in woven check gingham of polyester and cotton. $4.50 [$10-12] **Shoes,** cotton upper, vinyl sole. $3.50 [$10-12] **The Print shirt** in cotton, rayon, and polyester broadcloth. $4 [$10-12] **Culottes.** Detachable button-off panel in front and back; culottes legs underneath. $5 [$10-12] **Flared-leg pants.** $5 [$25-30] **Back-wrap skirt,** A-line style. $5 [$10-12]

Step lively in the nonchalant good looks of Pant-Dresses. **Front-buttoned step-in** style of textured cotton and rayon. $9 [$40-45] **Dropped-waist** step-in style of textured cotton. Self tie-belt; back zipper, loose panels in front and back. $8 [$40-45] **Wrap-around** step-in style, textured cotton and rayon, concealed snaps and front zipper closing. $10 [$40-45]

Summer 1969

77

Dresses with built-in B-cup bras. **Floral-printed** cotton and rayon, shirred skirt, back has "double-breasted" effect; buttons to waist and snaps below. Built-in B-cup bra. $8 [$35-40] **Pants-style.** Woven plaid poplin of polyester/cotton, dropped waistline; box pleats, back zipper. $9 [$35-40] **White textured cotton** with rickrack trim. Button tab across back; back zipper. Built-in B-cup bra. $9 [$45-50] **Sandal**, leather. $6 [$22-24]

Peek-a-boo cut-outs at front midriff caught together with white rings, giant white flowers on hopsacking of rayon and cotton, back zipper. $12 [$40-45] **U-turn cut-out** in back with cross-over buttoned tab, cotton pique bib-front, woven stripes on polyester and cotton, back zipper. $8 [$40-45] **Slot sandal** uniquely strapped in leather. $7 [$20-22]

Summer 1969

Denim blue separates play along with a red bandanna print and a duo of knit pullover tops. All are cotton. **Denim jumper.** $8 [$40-45] **Print mini-vest.** $4 [$20-24] **Pants** feature groovy print tie-sash and flare-legs. $6 [$24-28] **Textured knit top.** White zinged with red stitching, red buttons. $4 [$12-15] **Culottes skirt** . $6 [$15-18] **Striped knit top,** back neck zipper. $4 [$10-12] **Jamaica shorts.** $4 [$10-12] **Bag and scarf.** $5 [$24-28]

Swinging mates. Hi-rise pants of cotton sailcloth; bands around wide bottoms; back zipper; back-buttoned suspenders. Shirt of white cotton broadcloth with blowy sleeves and big squared collar. $14 [$50-55] **Groovy duo** in printed sailcloth strikes a happy note with white embossed cotton. Wide-legged pants and tunic zip in back. $14 [$60-65]

79

Chambray country shirts. Color-mated apache style scarf with wooden ring. High two-button collar band; long point, wide spread collar. Solid or wide-track stripe. $6 [$20-24] **Flare bottom jeans** in popular canvas. Body line fit from waist to knee, then gradual flare. Permanent center crease. Stripe or solid. $6 [$40-45]

Embroidered posies prance down the front of this tunic, back zipper. Navy flare-leg pants have elasticized waistband. $15 [$40-45] **Spinning stripes** ring the tunic, tie-laced bow accents collar. Wide-leg pants swing out to a flare. $15 [$40-45]

80   Summer 1969   Fall/Winter 1969

Turtleneck pullover with knit-in stripes; zipper at back neck. $7 [$12-15] **Modified A-line skirt,** double-knit, tortoise-shell-tone plastic buckle. $10 [$15-18] **Cardigan jacket** with tortoise-shell-tone plastic buttons and buckle. $16 [$15-18] **Box-pleated skirt** with elasticized waistband. $12 [$12-15] **Tunic top,** V-neck; contour seams; patch pockets. $12 [$20-22] **Cuffed wide-leg pants** with elasticized waistband. $12 [$28-32]

DACRON

Items 1 and 2 are
Sears Best

Shirt-style pant-top in a nifty new print has a great tailored look. Button front and cuffs; side vents. $14 [$15-18] **Fashion-right wide-leg pants** with an elasticized waistband. $14 [$18-20] **Print tunic top** has a V-neckline and self tie-belt. Knit of nylon. $11 [$20-22] **Twill-look flared-leg pants** in double-knit polyester have an interesting texture, two-way natural stretch. $11 [$18-22]

Triple-knit long tunic of acetate and nylon, turtleneck, back-neck zipper. $9 [$18-20]
Flared-leg pants in black and white checks, double-knit of nylon and polyester. $10 [$18-20] Pant-top, screen-printed polyester, with turtleneck, back neck zipper. $10 [$18-22]
Trim straight-leg pants in double-knit nylon. $8 [$15-18]

The nylon fiber in Pants 6 and 8 is
DU PONT
NYLON

Shaped jacket with notched collar; button-front; uncut cotton corduroy. $11 [$12-15]
Skirt with western flavor follows the A-line. $7 [$12-15] Knit shirt sports a couple of cartridge-style pockets, button cuffs. Cotton. $7 [$18-20] Lanky jeans of uncut cotton corduroy. $8 [$20-22] Surah blouse with sash, acetate. $7 [$12-15] Peppy pantshift of uncut cotton corduroy. $10 [$20-24]

Note: The flared-leg pants are the most popular pants style for vintage collectors. Recent redesign of the style has fueled interest in the late 1960s vintage.

VESTED INTEREST

SLINKY LOOK

Coin belt

Wear-Dated® item 4 is guaranteed to give normal wear for 1 full year or return for replacement or refund

Long sweater vest gives your midriff a ribbing. Wooden buttons; knit of acrylic. $9 [$20-24] **Glen plaid pants** sport wide legs that end in a flare. Woven of nylon, wool, and acrylic bonded to acetate tricot. $9 [$18-20]

White tunic shirt shaped in crepe of acetate and nylon. Tie-belt; back yoke. $8 [$20-22] **Double-knit pants** of acrylic. Wide flare-legs. $9 [$18-20] **Coin belt** worn here as necklace. $10 [$12-15]

Junior Bazaar

ON SAFARI

THE DANDY

Left: Bush Shirt. Broadcloth of polyester and cotton. $6 [$12-15] **Woven menswear plaid pants,** wool, straight-legs; waistband; belt loops; side-seam pockets, back pockets; zipper fly-front. Cotton lined. $10 [$12-15]
Right: Gold vest in cotton velveteen. $10 [$20-22] **Oxford-gray pants** with wide straight legs, bonded to acetate tricot. $9 [$18-22]

Left: Tunic over pants in acetate and rayon crepe. $18 [$40-45] **Thirties flare** in a flippy dress of acetate and rayon crepe. $17 [$35-40] **Lined bolero** of cotton velveteen with silver-color braid curves over dress of acetate and rayon crepe bonded to acetate tricot. Tie-sash; back zipper. $20 [$35-40] **Victorian charmer.** Empire-high acetate and rayon skirt bonded to a bodice of white pleated nylon. Trimmed with ribbon, bows, buttons. $18 [$30-35] **Slinky fish jewelry.** Bracelet. $6 [$15-18] Belt. $10 [$12-15]

Right: Textured double-knit polyester dresses keep their great shape. **Cream front-yoke** shoots straight up to a funnel neckline on easy-fitting skimmer. Back zipper. $14 [$40-45] **Zip-front dress** all checked out. $14 [$35-40] **Front-belt** buckles down a shapely-seamed skimmer. $14 [$40-45] **Long scarf** of rayon and silk twill. About 15 x 44 inches. $3.50 [$18-20]

The corduroys. **Curvy vest** sports clip-on gold-color chain. $8 [$18-20] **Striped turtleneck pullover,** back neck zipper, cotton knit. $5 [$12-15] **Pleated-front shirt** in white batiste of polyester and cotton. $6 [$8-10] **A-line skirt.** $6 [$12-15] **Leather-look jacket.** Textured vinylized polyester on cotton back. Collar and trim of curly polyester pile. $15 [$40-45] **Flare-leg pants.** $6 [$18-22] **Suspender wrap jumper.** $9 [$22-24]**Long Scarf** of paisley print, silk twill. About 11 x 41 inches. $3 [$15-18]

Note: Plaids were very popular in the late 1960s. Collectors tend to stay away from the more conservative or "classic" plaids, looking for "different" styles, such as the vest or flare-leg pants.

Pullover sweater knit of acrylic. Mock turtleneck. $9 [$8-10] **Plaid cuffed pants** with a dashing flare. $12 [$18-22] **Plaid jumper** with a Kiltie-look. Buckled vinyl tab; side fringe. Back zipper. $13 [$24-28] **Vest** of black cotton velveteen. $9 [$20-24] **Blouse** of white triacetate crepe. Lace frills detachable jabot and long sleeves. $7 [$8-10] **Plaid wrap kilt,** back pleats, side fringe; safety pin. $10 [$12-15]

The pea jacket in melton cloth of reprocessed wool, silk, and nylon. $18 [$30-35] **Flare-leg jeans** of midwale cotton corduroy, front zipper. $6 [$18-22] **Beret** with pompon atop. $2.50 [$12-15] **Scarf,** 6 feet long, 10 inches wide. $4.50 [$12-15] **C.P.O. jacket.** Woven tattersall check. $13 [$30-35] **Solid** color cotton denim flare-leg pants. $5 [$18-22]

Tweed-textured separates of acrylic and rayon. **Jacket.** Subtle cutaway style; back pleats. Lined. $19 [$20-22] **Pants.** Straight-leg style. $13 [$12-15]

Shirt in crinkle crepe of polyester and rayon. Neckband collar; saddle-shoulder. $8 [$8-10] **Skirt.** A-line style. $10 [$8-10] **Shift.** Piping detail; all-around yoke; back zipper. $20 [$15-18] **Coat.** Gentle seaming; all-around yoke; back pleat. Lined. $30 [$40-45]

Spring/Summer 1967

Unbeatable boy suit. Wool woven plaid. $20 [$35-40] **Blazer suit** in wool flannel, fully lined with paisley print of rayon taffeta. $22 [$35-40]

Plaid chesterfield A-line pairs handsome wool-and-nylon fabrics bonded to fusible cotton backing; has belt and inverted pleat in back; fully lined. $38 [$55-70] **Heather tweed cadet coat** in wool-and-nylon fabric. Fitted via "railroad track" welt seams in front; center seam and pleat in back. Metal-insulated acetate satin lining. $40 [$45-50]

88

Note: The "boy suit" came into fashion in the late 1960s. Most of the suits were single breasted with A-line skirts. Accessories often included pseudo driving gloves in soft kid. Many suits came with matching pants. We were about to turn an important fashion corner—women wearing pants on the job. The first steps in this were the pant suit and "pantdress."

Cavalry-look suit takes command in twill of rayon, nylon, and acetate. $30 [$45-50]

Bonded wool outfits. **Jacket, skirt, and pants.** Lengthier double-breasted jacket features mock-pocket flaps in front, dashing belt in back. $36 [$45-55] **Coat and dress ensemble.** Skim-shaped coat and turtleneck dress. $40 [$40-50]

"**Bubble**" **toque hat** in ribbed twill fabric of polyester and rayon. $5 [$12-15] **Diagonal-tweed** back-belted skimmer coat of rayon, wool, acetate, and nylon; lined. Shapely dress of wool and nylon zips in back. $38 [$55-65 set] **Diamond-pattern coat**; homespun-look dress of reprocessed wool, nylon, and other fibers; acetate taffeta lined. $50 [$55-65 set]

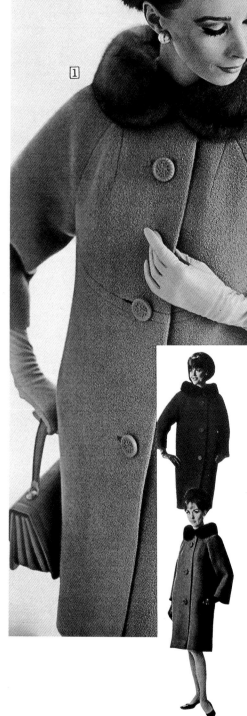

Collar of natural mink on coats tailored in wool-and-nylon fabrics bonded to cotton for shape-retention. Crepe-back satin linings of acetate and rayon. **Gently-shaped coat** with enviable double-stitched seaming. $67 [$65-70] **Easy, straight-away coat** with L-shaped seams that end in deep pockets. $67 [$45-50]

Note: During the late 1990s, fur-trimmed coats made a serious comeback. The vintage coats with fur collars did surprisingly well. Generally the vintage market for fur is not strong.

Dyed squirrel wedding band collar coat in bouclé. $45 [$45-55]
Dyed mouton lamb collar and cuffs; coat in soft, boldly woven fabric. $60 [$65-75]
Natural mink wedding band collar; coat in soft, boldly woven fabric. $45 [$65-75]
Dome hat of wool felt. Veil. $5 [$18-22]

Top: Rain coats. **Rayon-and-cotton twill** reverses to colorful acetate print that matches umbrella. Both sides are water-repellent, have set-in sleeves and jumbo pockets. $14 [$28-32]
Crushed vinyl fabric imitates fine-grained leather. Double-breasted style to wear with or without self-belt. Warm zip-liner of acrylic pile on cotton back. $14 [$45-55]

Bottom: Richly patterned nylon laminated to polyurethane foam, full acetate lining. $20 [$45-50] **Military look**, water-resistant diagonal rib-knit of acrylic laminated to polyurethane foam. $18 [$30-32]

Note: Designers are always looking for inspiration when it comes to designing raincoats. The styles from the late 1960s have been some of the most creative in fashion history.

Rain coats. **Sailor-collared style** has a swing of snappy pleats and half-belt. Rayon-and-cotton twill. Lined. $14 [$45-55] **Multi-buttoned styled** with storm-tab collar and two pockets in broadcloth of polyester and rayon. Nylon-lined. $18 [$35-40] **Tent coat.** Rayon-and-cotton twill. Acetate lining. $18 [$45-55] **Bubble beret** of polyester and cotton. $3.50 [$18-20]

Three-button coat. Wool and nylon bouclé bonded to cotton; lined. $30 [$50-55] **Coat and dress ensemble.** Same coat. Dress of wool and nylon bouclé, bonded to acetate tricot, zips in back. $43 [$75-80 set] **Scarf turban.** Rayon and silk. $5 [$18-20]

Bonded wool-and-nylon coat.
Bracelet-length sleeves, hand-piped buttonholes, fully lined with acetate taffeta. $26 [$45-50] **Wool covert-type coat** fabric bonded to cotton knit. Lined with acetate satin. $33 [$50-55]

Cardigan-style coat and cowl-collared dress. Coat of acetate bonded to polyurethane foam and then to acetate tricot. Slubbed acetate dress zips in back. Both fully lined. $43 [$75-85 set] **Oatmeal tweed coat** and dress of cotton bonded to acetate tricot. $40 [$75-80 set]

Note: The midi coat did not "catch on" and it seemed to come and go in a season. Perhaps it was the length. Women did not like juxtaposed against the mini skirts underneath.

Gray-dyed rabbit collar and cuffs on charcoal gray coat are detachable. Fine wool and nylon fabric; acetate taffeta lined. $50 [$75-80] **Lowered waist** accented with welt-seaming; wool and nylon fully lined with insulated acetate taffeta. Wide notched collar above a dash of metal buttons. $33 [$75-80] **Paneled front** framed with welt seaming and topped with a stand-off collar. Coat of fine wool fully lined with acetate satin; warmly interlined. $45 [$65-70]

Pillbox hat. Rayon plush (cotton-backed) in a print that looks like expensive leopard fur. $6 [$35-40]

Softly gathered skirt of wool woven multicolor plaid bonded to acetate tricot. Back zipper. $11 [$20-22] **Cossack dressing.** High-belted coat of wool melton cloth fused to cotton back; acetate satin lining. $40 [$60-65] **Edwardian look.** Cutaway jacket and side-zipped pantskirt of charcoal gray acrylic, bonded to acetate tricot. Cotton broadcloth jabot ruffled in voile of polyester and cotton; hooks at back neck band. $25 [$60-65]

Coat costume. Dashing navy blue coat dazzled with chrome yellow dress. Sleeveless dress, A-shaped, zips in back. $30 [$65-70] **Three-part outfit.** Jacket, flapped, buttoned, back-belted, has acetate taffeta lining. Pants, slightly flared, and skirt have band-less top, back zipper. $27 [$85-105] **Tapered boot** with soft leather upper warmly lined with acrylic pile. Inside per, elasticized $19 [$55-60]

featuring the smashing

LEATHER-LIKE LOOKS

Buckle-belted dress of cotton suede cloth. Shoulder buttons, back zipper. $14 [$45-50] **All-girl cadet-look** in cotton suede cloth, jacket and culottes-skirt. $23 [$65-70] **Cotton suede cloth jumper** with crepe pantdress, hip-belted, back-zippered; becomes a skirt via detachable panel with halter neckline, button closing. Pantdress of acetate and rayon crepe. $19 [$55-65] **Vinyl vest topping** dirndl skirt of woven plaid of acrylic bonded to nylon tricot; and shirt in crepe of triacetate with detachable bow. $19 [$30-35]

Tan jacket, all wool worsted jersey bonded to acetate for strength, then lined with acrylic pile on cotton back for warmth. $30 [$50-55] Brown Perma-Prest® slacks. Trim regular, polyester double knit. $21 [$24-28] Brown shirt of polyester knit, high-rise, self-fabric collar has fashionable long points. $12 [$20-22]

C.P.O. shirt, nautically styled with trim anchor buttons on placket front, cuffs and on the two button-through flap pockets. Acrylic bonded to acetate. Hers: $10 [$18-20] His: $11.50 [$20-24]

JUNIOR BAZAAR

Above & right: Reefer coat with zip-in pile liner, tweed of wool-and-nylon bonded to cotton, acetate satin lining. $40 [$55-60] **The mini-coat** in fleck-surfaced wool bonded to cotton, lined with acrylic pile on cotton back; sleeves lined with quilted acetate taffeta. Groovy belt rides low. $35 [$65-75] **Woven glen plaid** of wool-and-nylon bonded to cotton. $45 [$55-60] **Light camel tan** wool-and-nylon, woven with a flecked surface, bonded to cotton. $40 [$45-50]

Left: Blazer, double-breasted, knit of acrylic backed with polyurethane foam bonded to smooth acetate tricot. Notched collar; brass-colored buttons. His: $15 [$30-35] Hers: $14 [$25-30] **Perma-Prest® slacks**, double-knit polyester in hound's-tooth checks. His: $18 [$18-22] Hers: $16.50 [$18-20] **Shirt, mock-turtleneck** style knit of acrylic. His: $8 [$20-22] Hers: $8 [$20-22]

COLD WAVE

Fur-flurried coat, rabbit collar and cuffs, brushed-surfaced wool bonded to cotton. $50 [$55-60] **Dickey** in a rib-knit of acrylic. Snap at back neck. $2.50 [$8-10] **Dandy coat** in subtly textured wool. $40 [$75-85] **Star-checked coat** is woven of wool, acrylic, and nylon bonded to cotton. $35 [$75-85] **Boot**, leather upper, cozy acrylic pile lining, inside zipper, top elastic gore. $20 [$55-60]

8 Dickey

5

6

7

All-weather coats. **Balmacaan,** polyester and cotton. Collar has storm-tab closing. Zip-liner. Sand, light yellow, or navy blue. $26 [$45-50] **Trench coat.** Poplin of rayon and cotton. Zip-liner. Light beige, light blue, or deep navy. $27 [$50-55] **Boy coat.** Poplin of polyester and cotton. Zip-liner. Putty beige, deep navy, or deep taupe brown. $27 [$30-35]

Tri-color ribbon bands are new-now. Poplin of polyester and cotton with water and oil repellent. Pile zip-liner. $33 [$45-50] **Updated glen plaid,** belted coat with vinyl trim. Zip-liner with sleeves of rayon satin. $29 [$55-60] **Safari-style coat** with button-trimmed pockets, belt. Oxford cloth of polyester and combed cotton treated to resist water and stains. Lined. Zip-liner. $33 [$65-75]

99

Chapter Four

Swimsuits, Play Clothes, and Beach Cover-ups

A long-tail shirt is cover agent for suit. Printed broadcloth shirt and bra of rayon and cotton. Cotton duck shorts. $16 [$40-45] **Merry mod** mini-skirt flings over yellow stretch nylon suit. $18 [$40-45] **Peek-a-boo smash** in white eyelet embroidered cotton; pink ribbon; lined. $15 [$45-50]

Striped tank suit with hip-rider shorts of stretch nylon, natural-line bra. Shorts have mock fly-front, striped belt reverses to navy. $19 [$40-45] **Rich "poor girl" suit** with two rib-knit tops of acrylic; camisole-bra buttons in back; pullover has bra that hooks separately. Interlocking knit pants. $15 [$35-40] **Tropical print suit** and pants in textured fabric of polyester, acetate, and linen. $15 [$40-45]

Tapered-leg suit in woven cotton plaid with tracings of a jacquard design. Cotton lining. Inner bra with lace-lined pre-formed cups. $19 [$40-45] **Shirred sheath**, inner bra; suit may be worn strapless; back zipper. Elasticized bengaline of acetate, cotton, and rubber. $19 [$40-45]

Suit with floral appliquéd V-neckline in front; low back. Shaped inner bra. Tummy-control panel. Textured stretch-knit of acrylic, nylon, and rubber. $15 [$40-45] **Stretch nylon knit** with soft bodice and elasticized waistline. Tie-belt included. $15 [$35-40]

Terrycloth jacket of absorbent white cotton with crochet-look trim. $5 [$20-24]

STRETCH DUPONT NYLON

Jacket edged with white eyelet-embroidered ruffles. $8 [$18-20] **"Jeunesse" suit**, a flattering skirted style with white eyelet-embroidered insert; back zipper. $18 [$45-50] **Two-piece suit.** Camisole bra and boy-leg briefs. $16 [$45-55] **Pull-on pants** with white eyelet-embroidered flounce. $10 [$65-85]

Note: Swim dresses, such as the princess style "Baby Swimdress" shown, were very popular in the late 1960s. The matching pants were often bikini style.

Rib-tickler suit. White cotton pique bra, lined boy-leg pants, checked gingham of polyester and cotton. $13 [$35-45] **Bikini-style** with mad multicolor daisy print on cotton. Lined. $11 [$40-45] **Over blouse suit.** Striped top knit of nylon and polyester; orange nylon knit pants. $15 [$30-35] **Boy-leg suit** knit of acrylic, nylon, and spandex. Button-back bra. $11 [$40-45] **Baby swim dress** in two parts. Empire-look top, lined pants. Cotton with embroidered daisies. $16 [$30-35] **The Cap.** Rubber. Yellow with orange trim. White with black trim. $2 [$40-45]

Spring/Summer 1968

Sleek two-piece nylon knit swimsuit combines black-and-white floral print pullover-top with black pull-on boy-leg trunks; inner bra. $16 [$35-40] Two-piece hip rider swimsuit in stretch nylon knit; maillot trunks. $13 [$45-50] Shirred sheath stretches to fit all torso lengths; camisole neckline, zippered back; adjustable straps; inner bra. Elasticized bengaline of acetate, cotton, and rubber. $19 [$40-45]

Note: Collectors love the two-piece hip rider swimsuits from the late 1960s with plenty of "flower power."

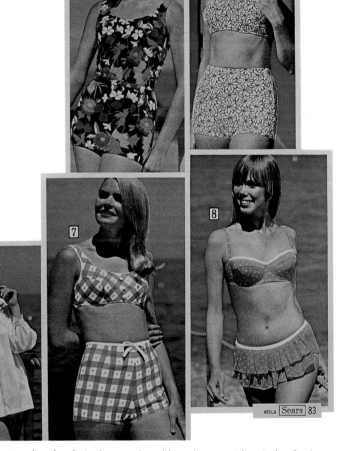

Floral print on stretch nylon knit. Scooped neckline dips semi-low in back; tie belt; inner bra. $16 [$25-30] Dramatic two-piece swimsuit is acrylic, nylon, and rubber. $13 [$40-45] Beach jacket. Cover up in white polyester and cotton. The push-up sleeves have button cuffs; tie-bow trims the neckline. $8 [$20-24] Two-piece swimsuit. Novelty-weave cotton gingham, back-buttoned bra. Shorts have back zipper, cotton panty. $18 [$40-45] Polka-dot print on voile of polyester and cotton; fully lined in cotton. Ruffles trim front of pull-on pants. $15 [$40-45]

Spring/Summer 1968

103

Three-piece ensemble of polyester and cotton. Pull-on ruffled bra-top and bikini-pants are lined with cotton. Ruffled jacket ties at neck. $7 [$40-45]

Dainty ruffled bikini on woven cotton and rayon, pull-on style. Bra-top has adjustable button straps. Pants have elastic at waist and legs. $4 [$20-25]
Wild flower bikini print on stretch nylon knit. Pull-on style. Bra-top has adjustable button straps. Pants have elastic at waist. $4 [$30-35]

Misses one-piece suit. Draped bra-section and over-skirt; boy-legs underneath. $13 [$45-50] **Men's shirt.** Casual beach style with Italian collar and four-button front. $6 [$20-22] **Men's trunks.** Zip-front boxer style; button-tab waist, elastic back. $5 [$20-22]

Note: The "belted look" with two-piece swimsuits became popular in the late 1960s. Bold prints, bright colors, satin, and flower power dominated the beach. Rubber bathing caps tended to be as elaborate as the hair styles they covered!

Girl's bikini. $5 [$15-18] **Little girl's bikini.** $2.50 [$15-18] **Little boy's trunks.** $1.50 [$10-12] **Juniors two-piece suit.** $10 [$40-45]

Glow-togethers of shimmery acetate crepe-back satin boast top-stitching detail, shiny globe buttons. **Roman-striped shirt.** Button-barrel cuffs, side vents. $10 [$20-24] **Two-piece suit.** Bra has adjustable straps elasticized back, button closing. Boy-leg pants zip in back. $15 [$40-45] **Petal cap** of rubber. $5 [$25-30]

A swinging trio so in tune it plays in four great combos. Cotton hip-rider suit and shift with vinyl tote bag. $15 [$45-50]

10

Daisy-dazzled swim dress of American dotted Swiss cotton. $15 [$40-45] **Lace hearts** ice this jacquard-patterned double-knit suit of acrylic, nylon, and spandex. Back-button bra. Boy-leg pants. $13 [$40-45] **White pin-dots** frost cotton print. Bra has tuck-away adjustable straps; elasticized back, hook closing. Lined maillot pants, ruffle-skirted in front. $10 [$40-45] **Baby blue bikini** of cotton embroidered eyelet. Bra buttons in back. Lined maillot pants, zip in back, elasticized leg openings. $16 [$45-50]

Maillot plunges deep down in back. Jacquard double-knit of acrylic, nylon, and rubber. $12 [$40-45] **Zippers trim this suit** of cotton duck. Bra ties in back; tuck-away straps adjust to halter-style. $10 [$45-50] **Winner stripes** in pebble-knit suit of acrylic, nylon, and rubber. $14 [$40-45] **Red stripes** cable-stitch knit acrylic pullover. Boy-leg pants knit of acrylic, nylon, and spandex. $15 [$35-40]

Flower power print three-piece set: modified bikini and a shift cover-up in cotton broadcloth. $11 [$30-35 set]
Sun checks. Three-piece set, modified bikini and a matching shift in woven cotton gingham checks. $10 [$30-35 set] **Bright stripes** in knit of acrylic and nylon. Two-piece suit. $9 [$12-15] Tank-style suit. $9 [$12-15]

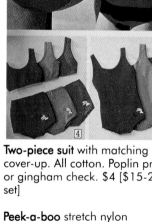

Two-piece suit with matching cover-up. All cotton. Poplin print or gingham check. $4 [$15-20 set]

Peek-a-boo stretch nylon Swimsuit looks like a one-piece suit from the front, a two-piece suit from the back. $3 [$12-15]

Belted stretch trunks set the pace for boys; rayon acetate and cotton elasticized with spandex. Nassau-length leg with surf style trim. Contrasting half belt plus buckle. $4 [$28-35] **Cotton crew neck shirts,** hemmed cuffs, bottom. Short sleeves. $2 [$10-12] **Cotton terry crew-neck shirt.** $2.50 [$8-10] **Trim-fitting trunks.** Stretch nylon, short Nassau-length leg. Drawstring waist. Inside coin pocket. $3 [$25-28]

Hip-length terry beach coat pairs with any kind of trunks. $3 [$15-20] **Heavy weight** cotton twill sharkskin trunks, solids with white trim, Nassau-length leg. $3 [$35-40] **Trim nylon trunks** have drawstring waist, striped sides. $2 [$35-40] **Cotton denim deck pants,** tapered calf-length legs. $2 [$25-28] **Bright boxer-style** cotton trunks. Plaid, elastic drawstring waist. $2 [$18-20]

Tropical print in cotton broadcloth, Bahama-length legs, drawstring waist. $3 [$35-40] **Reversible beach cap** flips to solid, cotton. $2 [$12-15]

Knit blazer shirt. Combed cotton. $3 [$12-15] **Form-fitting trunks** made of acetate, cotton, and spandex. $4.50 [$35-40]

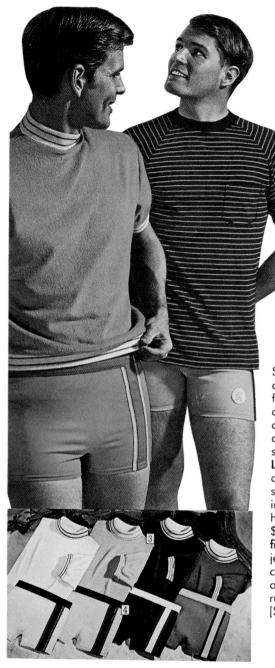

Sleek trunks with coordinated pullovers for men. **Casual shirt,** combed cotton chenille terry, collar and cuffs with double stripe. $4 [$10-12] **Low-rise trunks,** acetate, cotton, and spandex. Short 10.5-inch length, fit-to-the-hip for youthful builds. $4 [$35-40] **Form-fitting sets.** Fine-gauge jersey knit shirt of combed cotton. Trunks of acetate, cotton, and rubber for stretch. $9 [$45-50 set]

Summer 1968

Separates styled with go-together look for men. Nylon panel and stripe on front, back. **Surf jacket.** $9 [$20-22] **Trim surf trunks**, 16 inches long. $5 [$18-20]

Reversible kimono, cotton print reverses to gold-color terry, belt too. Pocket. $13 [$40-45] **Our finest trunks**, tapered zip-front boxer. Button-tab waist, tunnel elastic back for fine fit, zipper fly-front, 14-inch length, polyester and cotton. $8 [$15-18]

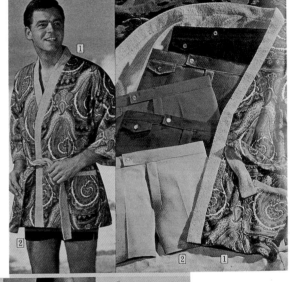

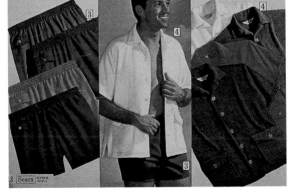

Boxer trunks. Polyester and soft combed cotton. Elastic waist, drawstring tie. $4 [$15-18] **Beach jacket**, cotton terry. $5 [$25-30]

Cotton coordinates, terry lined. **Beach jacket.** Two pockets. $89 [$22-24] **Boxer trunks.** Zip front; tab button waist. Pocket. $5 [$22-24] **Zip jacket.** Knit cotton terry. $76 [$30-35] **Boxer trunks.** Polyester and cotton. Zip front; button-tab waist. $5 [$18-20]

Striped two-piece swimsuit of crisp cotton sailcloth. Hip-riding boy shorts zip in front; front-belt. $11 [$45-50] **Slicker-style cover-up** in cotton sailcloth closes with gold-color metal clips. $8 [$22-24]

Three-piece set, yellow, green, and navy print cotton poplin. $16 [$55-65] **Three-piece set,** floral print on acrylic challis. Tunic cover-up zips at back-neck. $15 [$55-65] **Daisy print shift,** rayon and cotton poplin. $10 [$20-24] **Daisy print two-piece suit.** $13 [$35-40] **Dot-mates voile** of polyester and cotton. Two-piece suit. $11 [$35-40] Sheer cover-up, button-front style. Button-cuffed sleeves. $8 [$20-24] **Beach tote.** Cotton duck with white patent vinyl trim. $4 [$18-20]

Swimsuit, print cotton tunic-top styled with side slits, adjustable straps, back zipper, inner bra. Pull-on panty of double-thickness acetate tricot. $19 [$40-45] Petal swim cap, rubber. $5 [$25-30] Top-zip tote bag with double handle. Grained vinyl with patent vinyl trim. $3 [$20-22]

Button-trimmed suit of stretch nylon knit. $20 [$40-45] Suit of nylon knit in semi-high scoop back, adjustable straps. $22 [$45-50] V-neck suit in a stretchy knit of acrylic, nylon, and spandex. $15 [$40-45] Tennis-look suit in stretch nylon ribbed knit. $16 [$35-40]

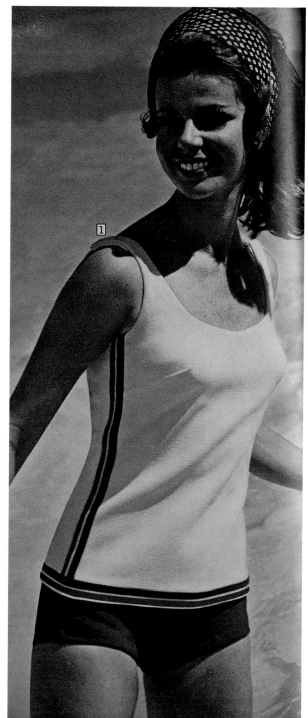

Look of patent on bold belted suit. Acrylic, nylon, and spandex. Crisscross-look bra buttons in the back; pull-on boy-leg trunks; black patent plastic belt. $13 [$45-50] **Yellow, orange, and pink** print bikini in stretch nylon knit, slightly shirred bra, pull-on maillot pants. $18 [$40-45] **Checkered suit** of nylon knit, bra buttons in the back, pull-on shorts have boy-style legs. $18 [$40-45] **Ribbed nylon suit**, pull-on trunks have boy-style legs. $17 [$40-45] **No frame "glasses"** made of plastic. $3 [$20-22]

Spirited suit in stretch nylon ribbed knit. Tri-color pullover top has adjustable button-straps. $16 [$35-40]

Nautical suit in stretch nylon knit. $20 [$30-35] **Beach-beauty suit** of nylon knit, black and white. Pullover top and boy-leg panty. $16 [$40-45] **Dazzle suit** of polyester top and nylon pants. $16 [$40-45] **Suit** of triacetate jersey. Pullover top has scooped back. Pull-on panty skirted with pleats. $23 [$35-40] **Tortoiseshell-color** plastic sunglasses. $3 [$20-22] **Swim cap.** Be the prettiest mermaid around in a fringe-and-petal-trimmed rubber cap with its very own blonde-color "fall" of modacrylic. $6 [$65-70]

Tiger-print swimsuit in stretch nylon knit. $13 [$65-70] **Jacket cover-up** comes out of the bush, cotton duck with a belt, shiny button closing, and button trim. $9 [$30-35] **Belted swimsuit.** Knit of acrylic, nylon, and spandex. $13 [$40-45] **Crinkly cover-up** in sheer and opaque striped seersucker plisse of polyester and cotton. Done like a snappy shirt with button-down collar, barrel cuffs, front closing. Side pocket to tote sun stuff. $10 [$20-24] **Polka-dot swimsuit**, cotton duck. $11 [$40-45]

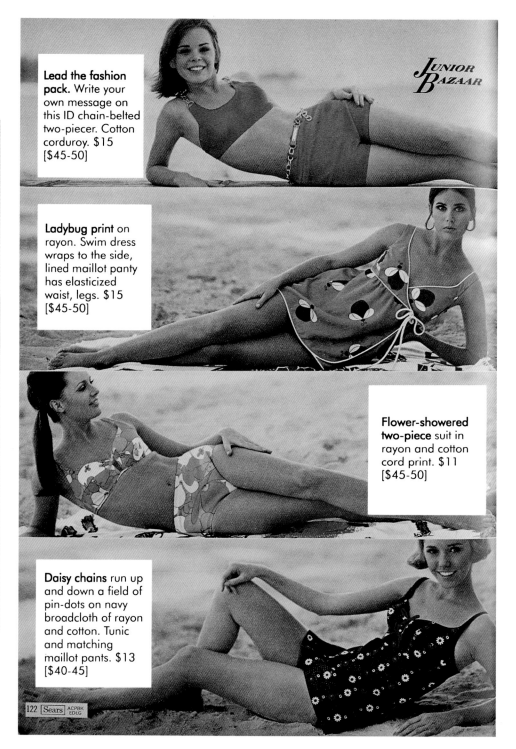

Beach Sets. Two-piece swimsuits with their own cover-ups. **Bright-white set.** Cotton pique. Button-back bra, button and rickrack trim. Cover-up has back zipper, button-straps. $19 [$40-45] **Ruffled-up set** of Leno-weave polyester and cotton. "Shirt" cover-up is see-through, has front buttons and button cuffs. $17 [$40-45] **Posy-print set**, cotton. $17 [$40-45]

Lead the fashion pack. Write your own message on this ID chain-belted two-piecer. Cotton corduroy. $15 [$45-50]

Ladybug print on rayon. Swim dress wraps to the side, lined maillot panty has elasticized waist, legs. $15 [$45-50]

Flower-showered two-piece suit in rayon and cotton cord print. $11 [$45-50]

Daisy chains run up and down a field of pin-dots on navy broadcloth of rayon and cotton. Tunic and matching maillot pants. $13 [$40-45]

JUNIOR BAZAAR

Surfing trunks. Cotton duck fabric. $3.50 [$45-50] **Pool pants.** Ideal for pool-side leisure. Fancy-fashion flared bottom. Cotton duck. $4.50 [$45-50] **Reversible beach cap** matches pool pants. $2 [$20-22] **Hawaiian bright trunks.** Cotton sateen. Jam styling, loose fit, longer legs. Assorted multicolor prints. $3.50 [$45-50]

Surf jacket. Long sleeves with elastic cuffs in exciting signs-of-the-times print. Cotton. $9 [$35-45] **Surfing trunks,** cotton; 16 inches. $5 [$45-50] **Beach pants.** Low slung drawstring waist with dashing flared bottoms. Cotton; nylon zipper fly, back patch pocket. Signs-of-the-times or multi-color print. $8 [$50-55]

Fitted-high, flared-low back-zip pants conceal a nifty two-piecer. Back-button bra. Lined maillot pants. Cotton duck. $20 [$55-60] **Cover skirt** hides a two-piece suit. Printed cotton duck. $18 [$45-50] **Double dipper.** Swim in a two-piece suit or attach the lined apron skirt and you're at sea in a swim dress. $16 [$40-45]

117

Chapter Five

Underwear and Nightwear

Note: Young collectors are buying vintage half slips to wear with cotton jersey shirts for day wear. Expresso brown is a fashion color that comes and goes on the fashion scene, but first gained popularity in the late 1960s.

White eyelet ruffles underscored with dark blue. Empire waist; full cut. $10 [$24-28] **Daisy bedecked,** sunshine-bright robe with contrast piping, front zipper. $9 [$18-20] **Crazy quilt** with blue-and-white stripes and checks paired up for a teeny bop-op look. Front zipper has swinging tassel. $8 [$32-35] **English school girl look** print robe, accented with a big blue bow and Peter Pan collar. $10 [$18-20] **Princess-style robe** gently hugs waist, thanks to hidden elastic in back. Zipper front, Peter Pan collar. $10 [$32-35]

Figure-fitting bodice, regular or mini length. Slips have lace around top, hem, bodice trimmed with water-lily embroidered appliqué. Regular lengths. $5 [$15-18] Mini (mid-thigh) length. $4 [$15-18] **Our finest slip,** empire-style fitted bodice of lace lined with sheer nylon. $7 [$15-18] **Expresso brown** is this season's hottest fashion color. Nylon tricot richly trimmed with creamy appliqués and nylon lace. Slip. $6 [$22-24] Pettislip. $4 [$15-18] Brief. $1.50 [$15-18]

Looks for the slumber scene. **Wedding dress look.** Lace edges; batiste, polyester, and cotton. $5 [$24-28] **Peek-a-boo look** in woven-check gingham of cotton with lace and ruffles. Leg openings of new peek-a-boo pants trimmed with three more rows of lace. $5 [$28-32] **Empire look.** Peignoir set with coat of woven cotton. Gown is cotton batiste with eyelet embroidery and trim at bodice, sleeves. $11 [$15-18] **Mini-shift look** with matching panties. Cotton broadcloth. $4 [$18-20] **Jungle print** trims cotton flannelette with brief panties. $4 [$24-28] **Matching knee-high boots.** $2 [$20-22] **The lithe lean look** in nylon leotard-pajamas and hip-length top. Acetate and nylon. $6 [$20-24]

Natural or contour cup bra. Nylon, spandex side, back panels. $2.75 [$12-15] **Matching half-slip,** 18 inches, nylon tricot. $3 [$12-15] **Chemise mini-slip.** Spaghetti straps, lace trim, nylon tricot. $4 [$20-22] **Long-leg** with front, back, and side self-panels. $5 [$12-15] **Brief.** $3 [$8-10] **Half-slip.** Scalloped hem-line with contrasting trim. Nylon tricot. $2 [$8-10] **Bikini brief.** Nylon tricot. Three for $2 [$NPA]

Cool cotton and cotton-blend nightwear. **Romper pajama** of cotton batiste, embroidered flounces down the front. $3.50 [$18-22] **Culottes** of combed cotton and polyester. Collar-less, sleeveless. $5 [$24-28] **Short culottes** with a crisp pointed collar and front placket. Windowpane check design. $3 [$15-18] **Mini shift** with ruffle at leg openings. $3 [$12-15] **Short culottes,** nylon zipper front, flounce at each leg opening. $3 [$12-15] **Peek-a-boo pajama** trimmed with band of eyelet embroidered cotton. $3 [$12-15]

COOL Cotton and cotton-blend Nightwear
In sizes Petite thru Large

SHORT story

JUNIOR BAZAAR

Taxipant bloomers. Nylon tricot, cotton lace. $2 [$12-15] **Lace-trimmed half slip.** Nylon tricot. 17-inches. $3.50 [$10-12] **Culottes pettipant.** Nylon tricot. $3 [$12-15]

Wee slip, nylon tricot. Subtle crepe-like texture. 27-inch length. $4 [$15-18] **Contour bra.** $3 [$20-24] **Bikini.** Nylon tricot. $1 [$8-10] **Half slip.** 17-inch length. $2.50 [$18-20] **Mini chemise slip.** 27-inch length. $4 [$24-28]

Karate lounge pajamas. Metallic gold print top contrasts with solid black pants. Cotton broadcloth. $6 [$40-45]

Cossack Style Pajamas for lounging, sleeping. Polyester and cotton. $8 [$45-50]

Hostess gown of satin voile, deep plunging back, contour bra. $23 [$45-50] Hostess culottes of satin. Built-in contour bra, satin bow at empire waist. Polyester and cotton voile, fully lined with cotton batiste. $23 [$45-50]

Lightly shaped brief of soft power-sheen elastic (nylon, spandex) feels like silk. White nylon stretch lace trims leg-band. $4 [$10-12] **Contour stretch bra.** Cups and front frame of nylon tricot with scalloped lace trim. $3.50 [$NPA] **Panty** of smooth nylon, spandex. Lace trim. $5 [$8-10] **Nylon tricot bikini.** $1.50 [$8-10] **Nylon tricot half slip.** 16-inch length. $3.50 [$12-15] **Nylon tricot mini chemise slip.** 27-inches from top of lace to hem. $4.50 [$15-18]

Non-cling slip of polyester tricot has special finish to reduce static electricity. $3.50 [$8-10] Bra-slip. Mini-length. $6 [$18-22]

THE "DOESN'T" SLIP™

of NON/CLING™ tricot

..doesn't cling, creep, twist

The Crepeset®
Bra-Slip

Half slip, broadcloth of polyester, and cotton. 16-inches. $3 [$12-15] Half slip, nylon tricot, trimmed with floral embroidery and lace, 16-inch length. $3 [$10-12] Culottes pettipant, nylon tricot. Lace trim, floral appliqué, 16-inches. $3 [$10-12]

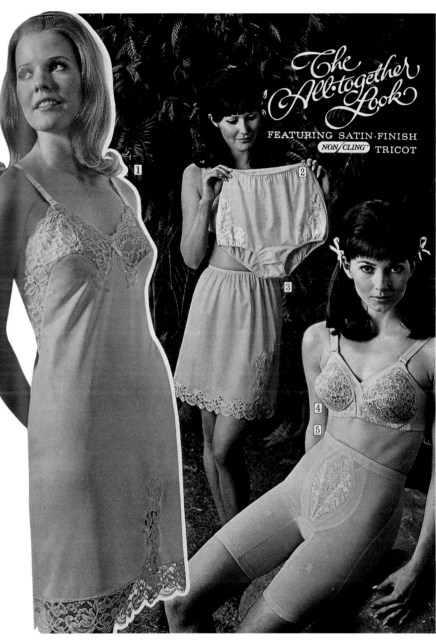

The All-together Look

FEATURING SATIN-FINISH
NON/CLING™ TRICOT

Non-cling slip, trimmed with lace, lined with sheer tricot. $9 [$12-15] Non-cling brief. Elastic leg. $3 [$8-10] Non-cling half slip. Lace trim. $6 [$12-15] Bra. Lined nylon lace cups edged with elastic for adaptable fit. $5 [$NPA] 19 inch long-leg panty girdle. $10 [$NPA]

Culottes with built-in bra. Jersey knit of triacetate. Silk-screened animal print. Bodice has cotton lining. $10 $45-50] **At-home gown** with necklace collar. Soft fleece of triacetate and nylon, gold-color mesh, simulated pearls, rhinestones. Butterfly sleeves edged with gold-look piping. $17 [$20-25] **At-home gown** with quilted skirt. Bodice of soft acrylic jersey bonded to acetate tricot. $20 [$30-35] **Culottes** with mesh belt. Soft fleece of triacetate and nylon. Front zipper with gold-color tassel. $15 [$40-45]

Chapter 6

Accessories

Quilted envelope in soft vinyl. Chain handle converts to a shoulder strap. $6 [$20-24] Pocketed pouch of top-grain cowhide. Top zipper, rayon lining. $9 [$20-24] Double-flap bag of grained vinyl. Strap adjusts from shoulder to hand size. $4 [$30-35] Mini-bag, shoulder-strap style of top-grain cowhide. $8 [$30-35] Buckle bag in top-grain cowhide with an adjustable shoulder strap. $9 [$30-35] Swagger pouch with a softly shirred pocket at each side of the gold-color metal frame. Crushed vinyl; cotton-lined. $5 [$20-24] Spacious tote with zippers on sides and top, grained vinyl. $6 [$35-40] Swagger pouch in grained vinyl. $6 [$25-30] Travel tote of grained vinyl. $4 [$20-22]

Neon-look raincoat in bright iridescent pink accented with shiny white, geometric-patterned pockets, embossed vinyl. Raglan-style sleeves. $6 [$20-22] Slicker coat, wet-looking patent vinyl, raglan-style sleeves. $7 [$20-22] Porthole umbrella, five see-through vinyl portholes, opaque vinyl cover. $6 [$20-25] Trench coat-look in waterproof vinyl with an embossed matte finish, raglan sleeves. $8 [$25-30] Umbrellas. [$NPA]

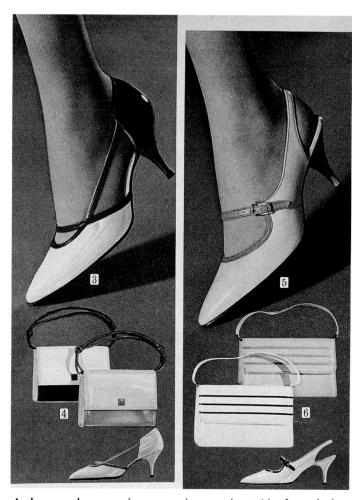

A play on color around curves and scooped out sides for a sleek, slim pump. Patent vinyl upper, 2.25-inch heel. $7 [$30-35] **Envelope bag** in patent vinyl with contrast-color fronts and handles. $7 [$25-30] **Tone or texture interest.** Uppers of soft leather or patent vinyl. 2.25-inch heel. $8 [$30-35] **Envelope bag** in smooth vinyl. $5 [$30-35]

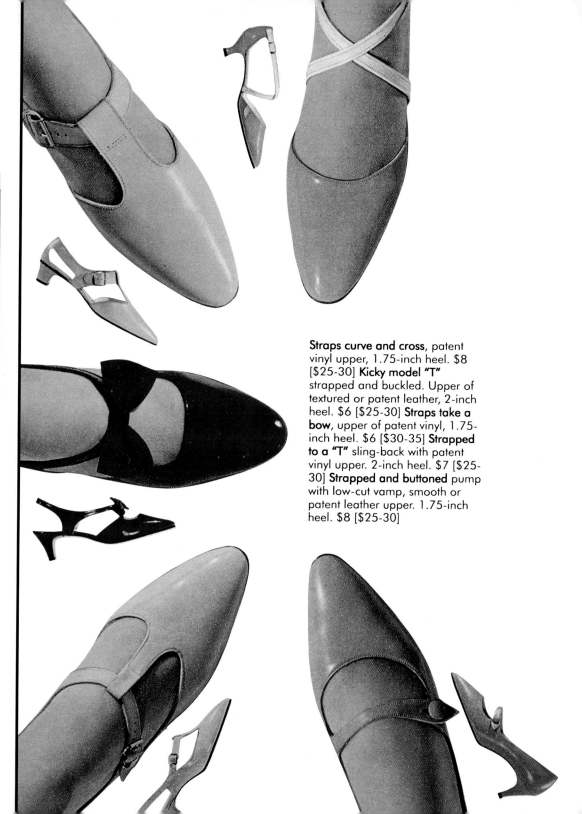

Straps curve and cross, patent vinyl upper, 1.75-inch heel. $8 [$25-30] **Kicky model "T"** strapped and buckled. Upper of textured or patent leather, 2-inch heel. $6 [$25-30] **Straps take a bow**, upper of patent vinyl, 1.75-inch heel. $6 [$30-35] **Strapped to a "T"** sling-back with patent vinyl upper. 2-inch heel. $7 [$25-30] **Strapped and buttoned** pump with low-cut vamp, smooth or patent leather upper. 1.75-inch heel. $8 [$25-30]

Leggy look based on heel exposure, instep strap, patent vinyl upper, 1.25-inch heel. $7 [$30-35] **Demure bow** on patent vinyl upper, 1.25-inch heel. $7 [$25-30] **Grained leather** upper with boldly crossed straps and a buckle perched on a brogue 1.25-inch heel. $8 [$30-35] **Vinyl upper** fashioned to a "T" and prettied with cutouts, 1.25-inch heel. $8 [$35-40]

Note: The concept of "cut outs" was not new in accessories' design, but the late 1960s pumps gave it a new slant. The shoes had a new lower heel, and the box handbag (popular in the late 1940s and early 1950s) came back into fashion.

FLASHY COLORS

ENTICING CUTOUTS

Crushed leather upper bares your foot through three side cutouts. 2.25-inch heel. $7 [$20-22] **Cobra-look cowhide** insert spices smooth leather upper, 2.5-inch heel. $8 [$20-22] **Suede upper** with smooth leather strap and bow. 1.75-inch heel. $8 [$24-28] **Envelope bag.** Grained vinyl, smooth vinyl handles and trim. About 8.5 x 6.5 x 3 inches. $7 [$20-22] **Box bag** of brushed vinyl, look and feel of suede. About 9 x 5 x 4 inches. $7 [$24-30]

Shoe with matching patent leather collar. 2-inch heel. $9 [$18-22]
Envelope bag of brushed vinyl has look and feel of suede. $7 [$22-24]

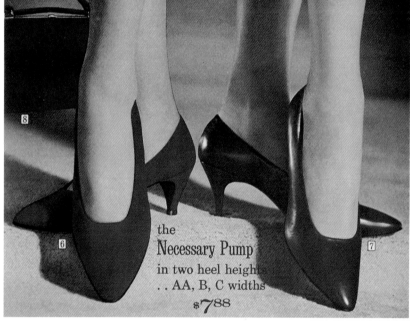

the
Necessary Pump
in two heel heights
.. AA, B, C widths
$7⁸⁸

The pump that takes you almost anywhere. Styled leather uppers in three finishes—smooth, patent, or suede. 1.75-inch heel. $8 [$18-20] 2.25-inch heel. $8 [$18-20] **Matching vinyl bag**. $5 [$15-18]

Intertwining hues on natural-color background bedeck rayon tapestry upper, 2.25-inch heel. $8 [$24-28] **Convertible shoulder bag** on a chain handle. Cotton, tapestry-print. $7 [$22-24] **Alligator-grained cowhide** upper with 2.25-inch heel. $7 [$18-20] **Tailored pouch** of alligator-grained vinyl. $6 [$15-18]

Note: Highest prices are paid for vintage shoes that were never worn or are in excellent condition. Styles that are "unusual," such as the "crisscross strap" style, are at a premium. Matching handbags add excitement for the collector also.

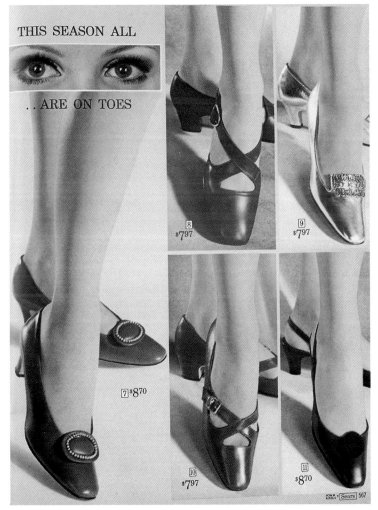

THIS SEASON ALL

..ARE ON TOES

8 $7⁹⁷

9 $7⁹⁷

7 $8⁷⁰

10 $7⁹⁷

11 $8⁷⁰

Sears 567

Studded bow pump with leather upper. 2-inch heel. $9 [$15-18]
Crisscross strap style in quality leather, 1.5-inch heel. $8 [$30-35]
Elegant pump, accented with high-rising ornament, upper is quality leather. 2-inch heel. $8 [$22-24] **Kicky young look** leather upper grained like kidskin, boldly strapped. 1.5-inch heel. $8 [$28-32]
Marvelous little sling features pert rosette on vamp. 2-inch heel. $9 [$24-28]

Kidskin uppers, nylon tricot lining, half-inch heel. $8 [$18-20]

Four-eyelet tie brushed leather uppers with bands of smooth leather across the vamp and around the sides, .75-inch heel. $7.88 [$18-20]

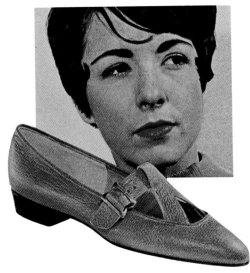

T-strap for a novelty turn in this lively buckled shoe with fine grained leather uppers, half-inch heel. $8 [$18-20]

Slip-on with kidskin uppers and burnished buckle, nylon tricot lining, half-inch heel. $8 [$18-20]

Fall/Winter 1967

129

Note: The so called "little shoe" and the low-heeled sling pump became popular and looked appropriate with the short skirts and A-line shifts. Shoes were styled in contrasting colors and unusual combinations of materials. Bows and other fancy touches began to appear.

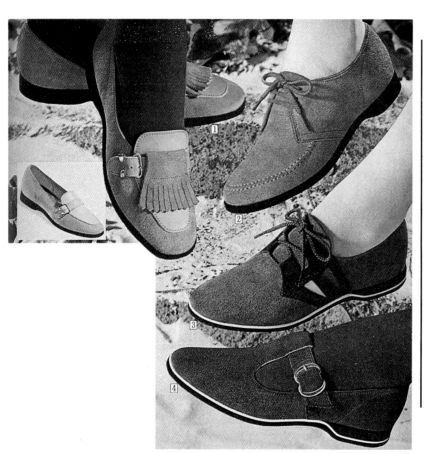

Kiltie slip-on, wear with fringe for a pert Scotch look or slip off fringe for a moc look. $6 [$20-22] **Moc-styled oxford.** $6 [$20-22] **Ghillie oxford.** Gray with colorful inserts in saddle. $6 [$20-22] **High riding T-strap.** $6 [$20-22]

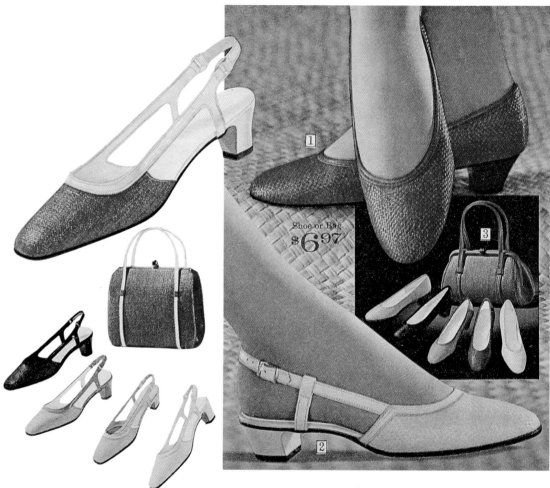

Shoe or Bag $6.97

Sling pump with straw and patent vinyl upper, squared toe and broad 1.75-inch heel. $10 [$24-28] **Matching purse.** Rayon faille lining. $10 [$20-24] **Fashion pump**, cushioned nylon tricot lining. 1.5-inch heel with a stacked-look. $7 [$20-24] **Perky sling.** Vinyl trim and adjustable sling strap, 1-inch heel. $7 [$24-28] **Handbag.** Roomy pouch-style in nylon straw-look. $7 [$18-20]

Two-toned leather uppers in daring color combos. $6 [$40-45] For a change of pace, a casual with pebble-grained pigskin upper and smooth leather trim. $7.88 [$20-24] Soft glove leather uppers, comfortable and lightweight.

Tassel 'n' tie glazed slip-on. $7 [$15-18] **High-rising vamp.** $6 [$15-18] **Classic moc-style.** $7 [$15-18]

Mad swirl of a bow on patent vinyl uppers. Square-cut throat. 1.5-inch heel. $8 [$24-28] **Handbag.** Double-flap pouch in patent vinyl. $7 [$22-24] **Crisscross straps** encircle the foot as only a sling can do. Patent vinyl uppers, 1.5-inch heel. $8 [$28-30] **Two-tone patent vinyl** uppers, peek-a-boo slit topped by a pert bow, 1.25-inch heel. $8 [$35-40] **Black patent leather**, one-eyelet tie, and spring's most vibrant hues, 1.75-inch heel. $8 [$35-40]

Pebble-grained pigskin with smooth leather trim. $8 [$20-24]

DENIM TAKES A BOW!

Denim takes a bow with cotton denim uppers, coordinated denim lining. $3 [$15-18]

SIZZLING summer SANDALS

T-strap with rounded toe, chunky heel, cut-out look. Patent vinyl, 1-inch heel. $6 [$18-20] **Barest of sandals** with glossy vinyl patent uppers. $4 [$15-18] **Criss-crossed strap** sling, patent vinyl, 1-inch heel. $5 [$15-18] **Snappy sling** has cool straw uppers, patent vinyl straps. 1.25-inch heel. $6 [$18-20] **Open-toed sling** pump with wide, grosgrain ribbon bow. Patent vinyl, 1-inch heel. $6 [$18-20] **Wide T-strap**, vinyl patent uppers, .25-inch heel. $4 [$15-18] **T-strap** goes dressy with a 1.5-inch heel, patent vinyl uppers. $6 [$15-18] **Graceful slider,** straw uppers topped with a daisy. $6 [$22-24]

THE SLICK WICKER-LOOK

Vinyl-coated rattan weave bags imported from Hong Kong. **Double-entry vanity,** leather and wood accents, wood handle. $5 [$24-28] **Double-handle** vanity, leather trim. $5 [$30-35] **Vanity pouch** with leather trim, rayon print lining. $4 [$24-28] **Duo-handle** vanity takes a trimming of leather, rayon print lining. $4 [$22-24] **East-west vanity,** double-handle style, leather trim, rayon print lining. $4 [$22-24]

THE SUMMER BAGS
romanticized with texture
$2 87 to $5 87

Wood beading, top-handle pouch, rayon lining. $5 [$35-45] **Hand-crocheted pouch** of rayon with the look of straw, rayon lining. $4 [$24-28] **Convertible strap** pouch in hand-crocheted rayon that looks like straw, rayon lining. $3 [$24-28] **Handy tote style** in wood beads and straw-look rayon. $6 [$30-35] **Convertible combines** wood beads, straw-look rayon, and metal chain. $4 [$30-35] **Swagger pouch** in hand-crocheted rayon that looks like straw. $4 [$25-30]

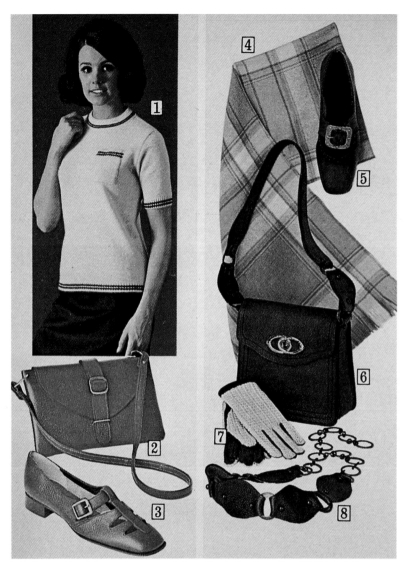

Left: Top with wide-track navy striping, flat-knit of acrylic. $5 [$12-15] **Shoulder bag** with gold-color metal buckle, top-grain cowhide, vinyl strap and tab. $4 [$24-28] **T-strap flattie** of grained leather upper, 3/4-inch heel. $6 [$20-22]

Right: Plaid scarf, about 14 x 64 inches. $3 [$8-10] **Slip-on** with buckled strap. Hidden gore. Leather upper, 1-inch heel. $8 [$24-28] **Shoulder bag** of top-grain cowhide, envelope style with saddle-stitching. $10 [$20-24] **Shortie gloves** of crocheted cotton with pigskin palm. $4 [$12-14] **Chain belt**; 39 inches long. $4 [$12-15]

Bouclé-knit pullover. $6 [$10-12] **Pouch-shaped handbag** with novel handle, top-grain cowhide, saddle-stitching. $8 [$20-24] **Scarf** in a vibrant print, silk twill. About 27 x 27 inches. $4 [$15-18] **Chain belt** with large medallion fob. $3.50 [$12-15]

Fisherman-knit pullover of acrylic. $6 [$10-12] **Pigskin gloves** with stretch nylon panels. $4.50 [$12-14] **Shoulder-strap bag**, cowhide. $6 [$18-20] **Snappy slip-on** with nail-head trim, leather upper, 1-inch heel. $7 [$20-22] **Chain belt**, ID buckle. $3 [$12-15]

Hardware trim on a high-rise vamp, perforated wing-tip design, 1.25-inch heel, leather upper. $8 [$18-20] **Puritan pump** with 1-inch heel, upper of leather and vinyl patent. $8 [$25-30] **Mini-boot** of stretch vinyl patent upper, bright buckle, 1.25-inch little heel. $8 [$35-40] **Turtle-textured leather uppers.** T-strap at the vamp, 1-inch shaped heel. $8 [$35-40] **Suede ties up** with patent leather trim, 1-inch heel. $8 [$35-40]

Mod three-eyelet oxford of brushed split leather combined with shiny patent vinyl. $6 [$35-40] **Swingy oxford** with bright hardware eyelets, leather or vinyl uppers. $7 [$35-40]

Fashion glasses with seven different-color interchangeable, break-resistant lenses to coordinate with your costumes. Plastic carrying case imported from Italy. $6 [$35-45 set]

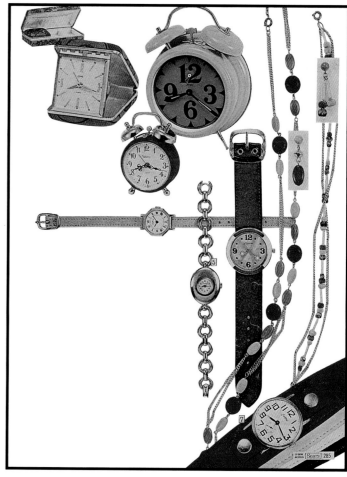

Alarm clocks. 40-hour key-wound movement; easy to see luminous hands, dots. $5-10 [$NPA] Ladies' mod watches. **Octagon shape**, gold-color base metal case; nylon strap. $13 [$10-12] **Chain bracelet watch** has oval case, safety catch closing. $17 [$10-12] **Flower power watch**, daisy hands mark time. $11 [$15-18] **Bold-faced watch** with four vinyl snap-on straps. $13 [$18-20] Necklaces and matching earrings. **Orange and green plastic beads**; gold-color metal. About 40 inches long; earrings about 1-inch long. $5 [$10-12] **Bone, beige, and brown plastic beads**; gold-color metal, about 54 inches long; earrings about 1-inch long. $5 [$10-12]

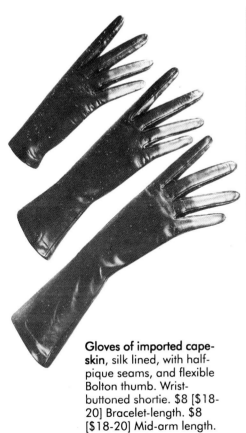

Gloves of imported cape-skin, silk lined, with half-pique seams, and flexible Bolton thumb. Wrist-buttoned shortie. $8 [$18-20] Bracelet-length. $8 [$18-20] Mid-arm length. $9 [$18-20]

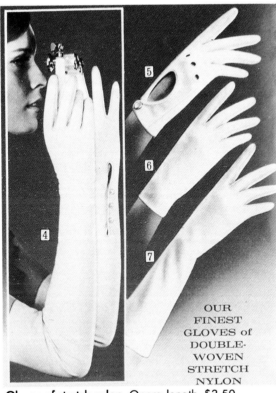

Gloves of stretch nylon. Opera-length. $3.50 [$15-18] Racing style. $3 [$5-8] Wrist-button shortie. $3 [$5-8] Elbow-tip length. $2.50 [$5-8]

OUR FINEST GLOVES of DOUBLE-WOVEN STRETCH NYLON

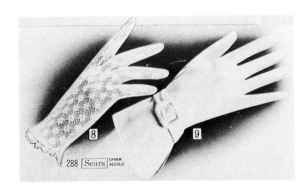

Lace shortie gloves of stretch nylon, delicately trimmed with scalloped cotton lace. $2 [$12-15] **Gauntlet gloves** with new buckle accent. Double-woven nylon, embossed for a leather-look. $3.50 [$12-15]

288 Sears CPBKM AEDSLG

1 The BARREL
2 The BOX
3 The SWAGGER
4 The SAFARI-LOOK
5 The VANITY
6 The ATTACHÉ

7

CPBKM AEDSLG Sears 289

Vinyl handbags. **Ring-trimmed double-handle** bag with gold-color accents. $5 [$24-28] **Top-handle style** with antique-finished metal frame and lift-lock. $4 [$30-35] **Pockets-a-plenty**, metal frame and trim on handles. $6 [$20-22] **Buckle-trimmed tote**, metal turn locks, top zipper, studs on bottom. $6 [$20-22] **Double-handle style**, metal lift-lock. $5 [$22-24] **All-purpose bag**, zips around three sides. $3.50 [$30-35] **3-in-1 Vinyl Tote.** Use it everyday as a pouch; snap it up to satchel-size for a more sporting look; use it as a tote when you travel or shop. Bone beige patent vinyl $10 [$20-22] White or black grained vinyl $7 [$20-22]

Vinyl bag. $8 [$15-18] **Smooth leather** or black patent vinyl upper, fabric bow, 2.25-inch heel. $9 [$15-18] **Patent vinyl upper**, 1.75-inch heel. $9 [$18-20]

Brogues with bold antiqued or pale leather uppers. **Two-tone tie** with antiqued stained leather upper, perforated toe, 1.25-inch stacked heel. $11 [$30-35] **Tri-toned Kiltie** with high-rising, perforated vamp, antiqued metal key-hole trim, wing-tip toe, 1.25-inch heel. $11 [$30-35] **Zingy wing-tip**, squared toe, sporty pinking, man-size perfs, 1-inch heel. $10 [$25-30] **Tomboy styling** in lady-like colors, harness hardware, bold perfs, and shadowed trim. $10 [$35-40]

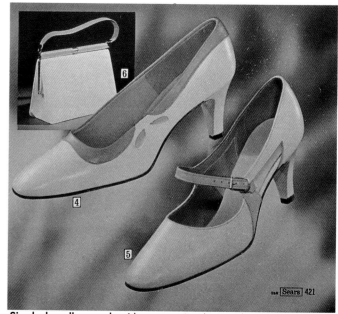

Single-handle pouch with contrasting bar and strap. $7 [$15-18] Smooth leather or black patent vinyl upper, contrasting collar, 2.25-inch heel. $9 [$18-20] **Two-tone leather** or black patent vinyl upper, instep strap, cutout sides, 2.25-inch heel. $8 [$18-20]

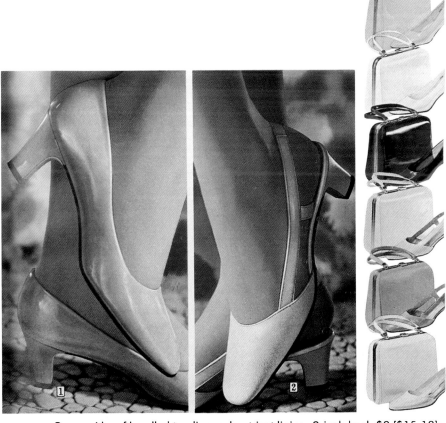

Pump with softly rolled top line, nylon tricot lining, 2-inch heel. $8 [$15-18]
Sling with elasticized strap, nylon tricot lining, 1.75-inch heel. $8 [$20-24]

Dressy Sandals
for carefree days and glamorous nights

Slinky leather straps uniquely interlaced for a "different" look, 1.5-inch heel. $9 [$24-28] **Bare little** stripping sandal with calfskin leather upper, 1.75-inch heel. $8 [$24-28] **T-strap** with contour-cut leather upper, 2-inch heel. $8 [$24-28] **Delightfully designed** with vinyl or rich leather upper, 1.75-inch heel. $8 [$28-32] **Latticed T-strap**, with rounded toe. Soft leather or black patent vinyl upper, 2-inch heel. $10 [$30-35]

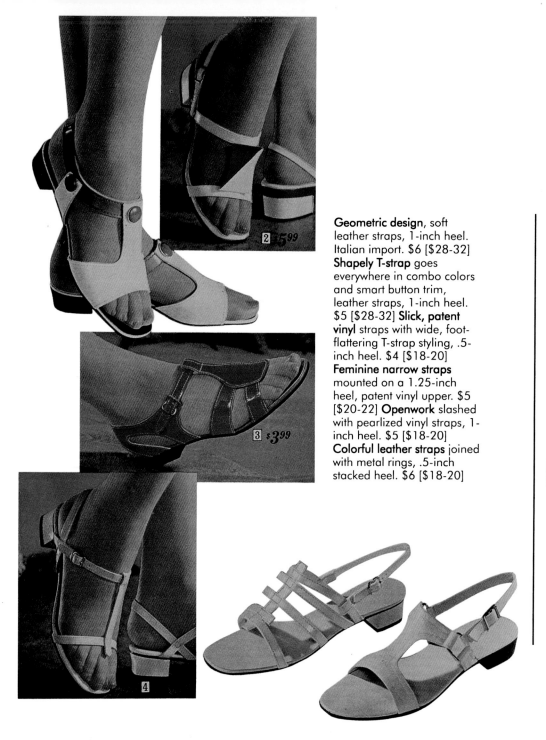

Geometric design, soft leather straps, 1-inch heel. Italian import. $6 [$28-32] **Shapely T-strap** goes everywhere in combo colors and smart button trim, leather straps, 1-inch heel. $5 [$28-32] **Slick, patent vinyl** straps with wide, foot-flattering T-strap styling, .5-inch heel. $4 [$18-20] **Feminine narrow straps** mounted on a 1.25-inch heel, patent vinyl upper. $5 [$20-22] **Openwork** slashed with pearlized vinyl straps, 1-inch heel. $5 [$18-20] **Colorful leather straps** joined with metal rings, .5-inch stacked heel. $6 [$18-20]

Pouch handbag in glove-tanned cowhide, buckle trim, top zipper, bottom studs. $16 [$40-45] **Shoes.** Glove leather upper, 2-inch heel. $16 [$40-45]

The vanity takes a trimming of nail heads on its double handle. $11 [$28-32] Pouch with front tab-trim. $8 [$30-35] Wide-strap shoulder tote. Tab closing. Welting accent. $13 [$30-35] Shoulder style in light brown has double strap and a top zipper closing. $10 [$25-30] Satchel pouch has a double handle, outside front pocket with turn-lock. $7 [$25-30] Tote sports a double handle, two large outside slip-in pockets. $15 [$25-30] Duo-handle satchel has gold-color metal ring trim. $9 [$20-25]

Spat in a combination of suede and patent leather, 1.75-inch heel. $15 [$30-35] Matching handbag. $15 [$35-40] Patent leather upper with rich sued insert, perforations, 2-inch heel. $15 [$18-20] Elegant metal ornament over suede leather onlay, man-made poromeric upper, 2-inch heel. $15 [$30-35] Matching handbag. $15 [$40-45] Classic pump with rolled top line, calfskin or black suede upper. 2-inch heel. $15 [$18-20] Matching handbag.. $15 [$40-45]

141

Note: Highest prices are paid for unusual styles, such as two toned, fabric tied, or two-strapped styles.

Patterned reptile skins in fresh colors. **Handbag in alligator**, metal frame, lock, and trim. $23 [$55-65] **Alligator upper** in two heel heights—2.25 and 1.5 inches. $23 [$50-60] **Handbag.** Lustrous iguana, double-chain handle. $23 [$65-70] **One-strap** styling crafted with iguana lizard upper, snappy scrolled brass button, 1.25-inch heel. $22 [$55-60]

Pump with iguana upper and fabric tie, high-rise vamp with elastic gore for good fit, 1.5-inch heel. $22 [$45-55] **Feminine-looking pump** with iguana upper, matching overlay with metal rings, 2.25-inch heel. $22 [$35-40] **Iguana envelope bag** with double handles, snap closing under contoured flap. $23 [$55-65] **High-stepping pump** with narrow twin instep straps. Iguana upper, 2-inch heel. $22 [$40-45]

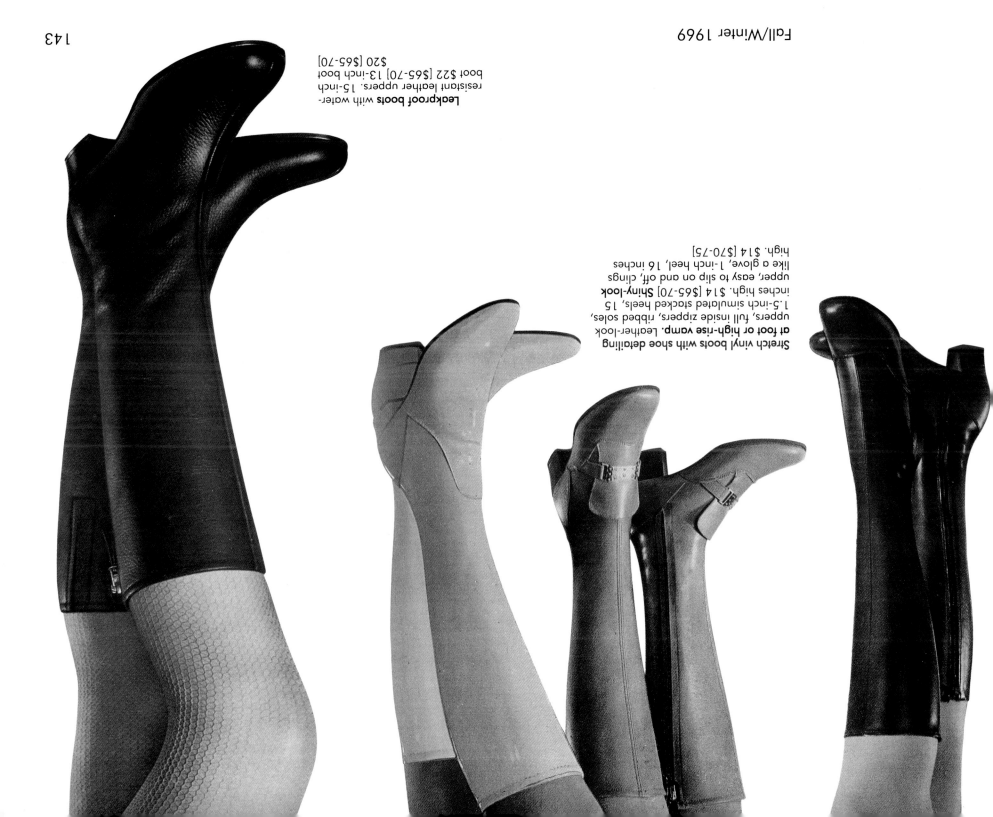

Leakproof boots with water-resistant leather uppers. 15-inch boot $22 [$65-70] 13-inch boot $20 [$65-70]

Stretch vinyl boots with shoe detailing at foot or high-rise vamp. Leather-look uppers, full inside zippers, ribbed soles, 1.5-inch simulated stacked heels, 15 inches high. $14 [$65-70] **Shiny-look** upper, easy to slip on and off, clings like a glove, 1-inch heel, 16 inches high. $14 [$70-75]

Slip-on with leather strap and twin leather keepers, high-rising vamp conceals elasticized gore. Smooth-finish upper. $17 [$24-28]

Wet-look wing-tip oxford with strap and metal buckle, leather. $17 [$20-22]

Wing-tip with metal D-rings, alligator print, high-rising vamp. $17 [$55-60]

Ultra-modern reptile print enhances leather upper, high-rise plain front. $15 [$55-60]